GENTLE DOG TRAINING

MICHEL HASBROUCK

Illustrations by BLANDINE HASBROUCK

Translated from the French by JEAN GILL

SOUVENIR PRESS

First published in Great Britain in 2007 by Souvenir Press Ltd,
43 Great Russell Street, London WC1B 3PD

First published in France in 2003 by Editions L'Archipel
under the title of *Dressage Tendresse*.

English translation © copyright 2007 Souvenir Press and Jean Gill

ISBN 9780285638013

Typeset by M Rules

Printed and bound in Great Britain

For Sultan, Oki, Udinette du Posty Arlequin, Pacha 2 des Hauteurs de la Sole, Retzi du Val des Hurlevent, Vlack du Domaine des Pins Noirs, Sioux de Naphil, Irok des 2 Pottois, Lutti, Oona du Dom Teckel, Cliff de Coblenza, Urane Bach du Graal, Barney Bach du Graal, Hero von Hirschel.

MICHEL HASBROUCK

For Stratos and his Vincent

JEAN GILL, translator

ACKNOWLEDGEMENTS

With thanks to the twenty thousand dog owners who, during these 40 years, have done me the honour of letting me train their beloved four-legged companions, and, nowadays, special thanks to the committed partners who have determined to become dog-masters in the growing world-wide dogmasters.com network I have created, and who will make my method live on well after I leave this world.

CONTENTS

INTRODUCTION

Canine Intelligence

Forget the bad old sayings

Let's take the bad old sayings and knock them on the head. 'Discipline and punish', 'Spare the rod and spoil the child', 'You have to be cruel to be kind', 'Don't praise your children – it will make them big-headed.' Society decrees a shocking upbringing for human beings and Jean-Paul Sartre was right in his statement that 'Hell is other people.'

This way of thinking – punish often but rarely reward – might work, in a fashion, in the human jungle, if we don't mention the underlying stress. After all, we have the gift of reason, we can mull things over and put them in the context of space and time. But our friends the dogs can't. When will we understand that, for them, these sayings are moronic?

If, instead, you really want to live on good terms with your dog, then forget the sour old methods of 'trial and error.' Why put the emphasis on 'error'? Far better to adopt a method of 'trial and success'. It's more fun, for you as well as your pet, and the results will be fantastic.

The dog is, in essence, an intelligence that serves Man. He was chosen by our ancestors for that very quality. He has a perfectly functional brain and he considers his master to be a genius. So make the most of this! Base your actions on the dog's intelligence, on his desire to be appreciated and loved, on his immense goodwill, not on his resistance to your punishments.

The aim of this book is to give you the right attitude in your canine relationships. The principle is simple; if you are pleased, say so. Right away. And fully. You can never give too many compliments to your four-footed pupil. Start with success. And if you're not pleased, say that too. But more quietly. And at once.

This need to respond quickly to a dog's actions is based on the consequences of one aspect of its intelligence. A dog processes information in the *present*. He cannot imagine himself elsewhere in space or time. His horizon stops at the *here and now*. You should never be late with a reward or punishment.

Take your dog to graduate level!

If you give your dog plenty of the information he needs, often, right from his early youth, you will develop his intelligence. Just like in humans, this works in the same way as a computer, by storing data and making connections as quickly as possible.

A dog's intelligence will increase with the stimulation of a broad cultural experience and he will rapidly learn to use this. This acquisition of knowledge depends largely on you. Your duty as a master is to enrich and develop to the maximum your dog's brain. An animal which has a variety of experiences, and which gets out and about, establishes crucial foundations in knowledge and his nerve systems respond accordingly.

These mental exercises are hugely important. Of course, it goes without saying that the body needs a work-out too. But that's something on which everyone is already agreed.

You have everything to gain from stimulating the intelligence of your dog. If he is nurtured and full of high spirits, he will possess two essential characteristics; everyone will love him and he will be comfortable in his own fur. And on top of that, you will be so proud of him!

Become a good master

From now on, get used to communicating with your four-legged friend with my favourite maxim in mind; 'A sentence intended for your dog should have a subject, a verb and a compliment!'

Of course, no-one becomes a top trainer after having read a couple of books on the subject. It takes years of work and observation, guided by experts, to gain training know-how, to handle any sort of dog correctly and to deal with every kind of problem.

It's a complex subject. Our four footed companion's instinct, fascination and mystery still defy explanation by experts.

There are, however, some universal principles. Some of them are ages old, such as those cited by the Roman writer a Columellus, or by the great masters of training nowadays, champions in the hunt, or with protection dogs, or in the more recent competitive sports of obedience, agility, flyball, dog dancing, dog teams etc. In the army, my tutor Sergeant-Major Schwartz told his young trainee dog-handler that 'training is not breaking-in'.

There are also more modern principles, particularly those established by English and American behaviourists, who try hard to apply their observation of animals to solve every-day problems, or to relate research discoveries about the human brain, to that of the dog. This work has been enriched by psychologists from various disciplines, from the school of Pavlov to that of Palo Alto, taking in neuro-linguistic programming and psychoanalysis en route.

Since 1966, I have confirmed the effectiveness of this understanding, adopting some ideas and rejecting those that seemed wrong to me. In this way, I have continually evaluated and improved my technique, without being seduced by fashions, and every day I try to pass on what I know to the public at large. Many thousands of dogs have passed through my hands and I am absolutely convinced of one thing; it is always possible to resolve difficulties, provided that there is the technical knowledge, the willingness to learn, and that the training takes place in an atmosphere which puts the dog at ease.

It is true that I have had thousands of normal puppies or dogs for training, with few problems, for the sole reason that their owners wanted a good start either for themselves as masters or for their puppies, or sometimes because they wanted help to solve, in the right way, some everyday problems that had cropped up.

But I have also worked with hundreds of more dramatic cases, extremely dangerous dogs condemned to euthanasia. Faced with these, I have had to prepare for full combat. In the world of hounds there are days when training seems more like rock n' roll. People who were there remember such days as epic battles between two terrestrial mammals, an enraged dog and me. With blood on the sand, generally mine.

Sometimes, I've even seen a few perverts turn up whose sole aim is to see me torn to shreds by their dogs, probably for a stupid bet with their friends in the local bistrot that my Gentle Dog Training would bite the dust in front of their wild animals. They've been surprised to lean, even if a bit too late, that in Gentle Dog Training, there is also training. And every time, it was vital that I won, without hitting, without shouting at the dog, which in any case had already seen more than its share of blows and bellowing before coming to me. For my objective was always the same, to save the dog and never to resign myself to accepting euthanasia as a fate.

So, from here on, I have arrived at the 'third stage' of my 'canine life'. After the phase of trials and championships, after that of working as a professional trainer, I am now training a team to use my methods. My aim, from now on, is to make sure that those dog-owners who so wish can find good guidance, calling on competent trainers in the regions where they live, without having to travel vast distances.

This teaching I'm involved in contains its own rewards and improves my own skills yet again. My students are highly motivated, they teach me a great deal and they challenge me with their astute questions and wide personal experiences of people and dogs, ensuring that I continue to progress myself, rather than slip into complacency.

My Method

Following one of my conferences in Liège, Belgium, in 2004, I was finally persuaded to define my doctrine. It is based on twelve points:

To create or re-create the dog's trust
- Lavish rewards on the dog when it succeeds
- Write off mistakes, without a punishment

- Don't hit the dog
- Don't shout at the dog

To be a traditional trainer still
- Demand proper obedience to commands
- Obtain this result rapidly
- Use the simplest training tools
- Outlaw all jargon and incomprehensible debates

And to really guide my clients
- Train the master carefully
- Turn down group lessons
- Offer revision lessons, free, for life
- And always work in a good mood.

Some of my stances – on the telepathic contact which should be established between human and puppy when the latter is still in the womb, commands given in a purring voice, or the need to look your dog directly in the eye – might well surprise you. But don't worry. The answers I offer are simple, effective and always morally acceptable.

This book is, above all, a method of dog handling, to which I've added some explanations as to what's going on, in my opinion, in the head of our marvellous four-footed companion. My aim is to better prepare dog owners so that you can lead your dogs and even, if you so wish, continue above and beyond a basic training.

The canine tom-tom

In 1998, I was invited to Togo to train dog-handlers for a security firm, set up by a French ex-military-policeman, a brother-in-arms. I had a little free time so I let it be known that I was willing to run a basic training class for dogs owned by the general public.

Over there, the tom-tom works well! One day, a charming lady turned up with a Bernese Mountain Dog, which seemed to have adapted very well to tropical Africa, but which was obedient only in frosty weather! I explained my programme to her.

Before deciding whether to take up my services, she asked, in a slightly anxious tone, 'You won't hit him though, will you?'

Calmly, I replied that I had stopped making that mistake a long time ago and that I had published a book in which I had collected numerous tips on dog training. The lady to whom I was speaking then said, 'You're *that* Michel Hasbrouck? It's your book? But I know it off by heart, it's my bedside reading. I've bought a copy for all my friends!' So it got back to me that I had readers in Lomé. On the Equator, in the middle of nowhere! Long live Gutenberg!

It is this very book, corrected and enriched, that you now hold in your hands.

Belgian Shepherd Dog

CHAPTER 1

Are you suited to owning a dog?

'I know I could never live without a dog'

JOHNNY HALLIDAY (ANTENNE 2, 2002)

Before getting a puppy, or a dog, examine your conscience. The question is not, 'Do I need a dog?' but rather, 'Could I make one happy?'

We tend to make use of the world around us, selfishly. That doesn't matter when it's only things that are affected. But this is not about a gadget. An animal cannot be compared with a toy. You have to respect it and understand its deepest nature.

This respect extends to all pets, of course, but perhaps even more so for the dog. Our brave *canis familiaris* has one special characteristic; he is one of us.

Every day you see the proof of that old adage, 'Like master, like dog.'

More than the cat, which also lives inside with us, but rather inside its own feline world, more than a goldfish or a parakeet, the dog puts us in touch with our prehistoric roots, with that period when we depended on him for food and survival in the face of our enemies. When, in those ancient times, Father *Erectus* offered his lovely Lucy a diplodocus bone, that his *Barophogus*, the guard-dog extinct nowadays, had perhaps allowed him to dig up.

Without a doubt it is the dog, more than other animals, which engages us in the study of its personality. Among the animals in our everyday lives, it is the only one that forces us to take a daily walk, regardless of snow or heatwave. He takes us out of our concrete towns. He gives us the opportunity to meet other dog-owners by chance on walks.

He is also the only household pet to accept training and he communicates easily with us. Perhaps he can't say many words, but he expresses himself perfectly clearly, and often. Experts in animal psychology have even dubbed him 'Champion of invisible communication'. He knows perfectly well, sometimes even when we don't, how to read our appearances and our smallest gestures. So if you want to buy a dog, it's not a spur of the moment decision. Not everyone is capable of owning one.

Telepathy

My dog Hero knows perfectly well how to distinguish between the days when I'm taking him out with me and those when I'm leaving him at home. All the same, I dress the same way, I take the same briefcase, I get into the same car. When I have decided he's going with me, he accompanies me to the car. Perhaps I seem more relaxed? I must give off a slightly different scent depending on my mood. When I can't take him with me, he stays in the house. And yet I don't say a word to him.

For my own part, I am convinced that dogs read our thoughts telepathically.

Brittany

Characteristics of a good master

According to all the studies, dog-owners are generous, even altruistic people. In general, they enjoy life. That said, we must remember that goodwill alone is not enough. Buying a dog brings constraints. Owning a pet means making a permanent effort. You have to control yourself, behave with restraint and justice, and not be stingy with your affection. It is sometimes very expensive, in veterinary fees and food bills in particular.

A consistent attitude is also necessary; the man or woman who is temperamental or unstable is never a good master for a dog. A secure base is imperative for dogs. Otherwise, look out for behaviour problems.

In consequence, as the experts like to say, 'When a dog does something wrong, eleven times out of ten it's the master to blame.' So, before you train your dog, learn to understand your own nature. This is not easy but others' observations can help in the task. If those around you think you're bad-tempered, there is certainly some truth in this.

Take your own personality into account but don't be scared to try a training activity in case you make a mistake. Today's error can be the foundation for tomorrow's success, provided that you recognize it and put it right. Too often, the beginner is unable to evaluate himself as a trainer. One objective of this book is to start off this process of learning.

The advice I'm giving you shouldn't hide the truth; I've made plenty of mistakes myself and I'll tell you about them. That way I hope to help you avoid the traps into which I've fallen. Each mistake you avoid is one less fault in your dog and it is always the dog that pays the price.

Chew it over

To train your dog well, use your mind and not your muscles!

This is a primordial principle; canine know-how, linked with affection, that is to say to a kind attitude which still carries authority, will enable any difficulty to be resolved. When you call on the intelligence and energy of your four-footed friend, you will recover from virtually any false step, especially if you began his apprenticeship at a very young age.

It is imperative that you win his trust. He must think, 'You are my master, where you lead, I follow and everything is provided.'

If your pupil defies you because you have put too many hard obstacles in his way, which have scarred him physically or psychologically, or because you have ill-treated him, then the apprenticeship will be difficult, particularly if your pet is sensitive. Not every dog has an irreproachable temperament.

You have to know how to progress in small steps, to take your time, and build without botching, so that, when necessary, you can always drop back a little, on familiar ground. Don't jump steps through impatience.

Many people resort quickly to punishment, to 'slippertherapy' and are stingy with caresses. In fact, the opposite should be the norm. Training, yes – and sometimes firmness – but paramount is 'tenderness above all else'. When the day goes badly, when you're irritated, when the dog retreats into its shell, the most sensible solution and the wisest for future success, is to stop everything. Take your hat, go out for a walk, with or without your dog, with no ulterior motive, all thought of training put out of your mind for the moment. Anger is always a momentary madness, the worst of counsellors.

If you have to resort to punishment, make it immediate, decided with a cool head, and stop, the moment your pet shows the slightest sign of goodwill.

Keep in mind that it is essential that you take care of him. He tires very quickly, this big ol' baby wolf that sleeps all the time when loose in the wild. If you work with a dog that has used up all his store of concentration, you risk destroying his learning. It's better to go out twenty times a day on a successful little walk of only a few metres, lasting one minute each, than to demand three kilometres on lead in one go during which your pupil, shattered, loses concentration at the slightest distraction.

Since Tristram's days

The basic mechanism of training hasn't changed since the days of 'Tristram and Ysolde', the medieval romance in which the hero teaches his pointer how to retrieve game; hit him to punish wrong-doing, a few rewards when he gets it right. Little by little, the dog learns to avoid punishments and find his own rewards by doing what he's allowed to, for example by running off to hunt without the hindrance of a master.

The mechanism at work in 'Tristram and Ysolde' errs therefore on two assumptions:

- The priority given to punishment; this is not my philosophy.
- The passive approach; it assumes that the dog is talented, that a dog from a 'hunting breed' becomes a hunting dog without being taught what to do. What if it's just your average dog? What do you do then? There is no answer. It's the dog that's useless, not the owner. In this method, you're allowed to maltreat him as he's deserved it.

This method is far too limited in technique.

Being precise

If, to get your dog to go down, you say 'Down!' one day, 'Lie down!' the next and 'On the ground' on the third day, sometimes shouting, sometimes whispering, one time standing straight as a post, another time leaning right down to the ground, in short, if you give your young pupil the very picture of an inconsistent master, you are putting in place all the conditions to wreck the training.

Certainly, lack of precision isn't always such a caricature but the results are always the same; it washes out the best foundations, the most perfect training, and kills, in embryo, the best will in the world on the part of your pet.

When training is well-established, then it is appropriate to raise the level of challenge. Then, it's a good idea to act in an unpredictable way, to make intentional mistakes, so that you can test how solid the consequences are. But, to start off with, you are not entitled to be 'more-or-less' consistent.

Use your memory to obtain this precision in your work. Thanks to this ability, you can recapture the next day exactly the same results you obtained in previous training. As soon as you have your first success, you can also vary the times and places where you train your dog. Keep a careful record in your head of all the details that made a difference, what made an impact, how your dog reacted to such and such an incident, what are his strengths and weaknesses etc. It's a good idea to take written notes that you can read over afterwards in peace and quiet.

You should imprint yourself on your dog, and have an intimate understanding of this extremely sensitive creature, this champion of subtle communication, able to decode your tiniest movement in the most astounding manner, and with his unique personality.

You don't work in the same way with an atomic dog and a couch potato. You have to know what sort of dog you have in front of you. Only love allows you to enter the mental universe of a dog, because with love comes the necessary perseverance, patience, interest, in short all the qualities you need to succeed in training.

Firmness

I've intentionally kept till last this word 'Firmness' which seems to have magic powers for so many who talk about training dogs. Those who mention 'training' often evoke images of whips, and ill-treatment. In their minds, there is always an association between training and firmness.

Meanwhile, at the same time, these same people are willing to exempt themselves from any mistakes. Let me emphasise one thing; a dog's master should show firmness, but above all with himself!

You can indeed show firmness to your dog, according to the old authoritarian principle; 'I've given you an order, you are capable of carrying it out, so you must obey.'

Authority, the framework of life

Well-established authority, clear and light-handed, radiant and peaceful, gives the dog a structure rather than frustrating him.

The dog, a hierarchical animal, needs to feel his master's authority over him. An authority which is calm, benevolent, serene, which creates a secure atmosphere in which the dog can express his personality, have fun and work, without too much stress.

The authority of a dog's master should be like that shown in the dressage ring by a great rider, who guides his horse through the most complex figures, without saying a word, in an apparently effortless display.

Firmness is not brutality, which is so often born from too permissive a beginning. You let your dog run wild then, one day, you are forced to discipline him. Far better to play the consistency card and always get the same reactions. A question of being precise, yet again.

Pyrenean Sheepdog

Always more to know

Armed with all these qualities, you are still missing one essential – the techniques.

It is absolutely primordial to seek information, ideas and advice. The tool most readily to hand is the book. It has the advantage of giving you information in peace and quiet. You can read, you can flick back and you can reflect tranquilly on what you've read.

Unfortunately, many authors have only a very limited experience of canine education and are contented to repeat the ineptitudes that they have read in works that are themselves a mere copy of others. No indeed, not all books about training are good ones.

Nevertheless, skim through them. You will end up sorting the good from the bad by the internal contradictions. In this way you will acquire a general background in canine studies, and you will forge an initial philosophy. But keep in mind that a book can't tell you everything. Each dog is unique, as is each master. Each dog/master relationship even more so. A book, however detailed it might be, can never take into account the complexity of all possible situations, nor say to you, on the spot, 'This is what you're doing wrong.'

I repeat this truth to all my clients, with regret, because I would dearly love to write THE definitive book on the subject. The one that would replace all canine experts. Mission totally impossible...

If you can come on a course with one of the trainers in the 'Dressage Tendresse/Gentle Dog Training' team. There, in a very short time – six hours spread over a day and a half – you will be given a personalised programme which goes a long way beyond the generalisations in this book. And I know that the technique works...

Working alone

Learn and keep learning. One day, you will be sure that you have finally understood the workings of your dog's brain and that you've grasped the principles of training. You can then move on to a more active, imaginative phase, of your own making.

And never forget one of my favourite sayings; no-one is born a good master; you become one!

CHAPTER 2

Choose your dog carefully

'To his dog, every man is Napoleon; hence the constant popularity of dogs'

ALDOUS HUXLEY

Specialists distinguish between ten groups by morphology and behaviour. In essence, you can narrow it down to three main categories; guard-dogs, retrievers and companions. Breeds are no more than different shapes and characteristics of these categories.

Clearly, a labrador can also be a good guard-dog, retriever and companion, but you might prefer a dog bred for the specific purpose. It would be a lot more accurate to talk about particular breeding lines rather than breeds. In practice, at the heart of one breed you will find everything and its opposite.

There are lazy German Shepherds and aggressive Yorkshire Terriers. The well-advised buyer, thinking of buying a puppy, will want to know all about its parents. A little Irish setter whose ancestors for ten generations have hunted nothing more than the flies which stop them sleeping peacefully on their cushions has little chance of becoming a good retriever in the marshes.

If they are not kept up, characteristics are lost. This goes for shape as well as character.

How to recognise a good dog

Many books present the advantages and disadvantages of different breeds. It's better not to rely too much on this when choosing a dog. Every breed is described as the most beautiful and the best, each as much as another. Again and again you read, 'Good guard-dog, friendly with children, excellent worker, this dog responds to training that is gentle but firm. Also, he needs exercise.' These are commercial descriptions, far too general to be useful. Don't believe everything you read. Find out more beforehand and read between every line!

Shun the scared dog

Since Desmond Morris brought out his work 'Dogwatching' everyone has known this; at heart, the dog is still a baby wolf, whatever its age, its colouring or its size. And the solitary wolf is a frightened beast.

When you come to choose the young animal, look for any lack of self-confidence.

If a puppy seems frightened, shun it. Even more so, if the whole litter is the same. The hidden vice here is called 'privation syndrome' or 'confinement syndrome'. The puppy has certainly been brought up away from people with 'hygienic reasons' as an excuse. It looks normal but it is starting life with an enormous handicap; it is upset whenever it is confronted with any small change, with unusual noises or strangers. Trainers know this all too well; dangerous dogs are all too often animals that are terrified.

Whatever might be the cause, avoid taking a puppy

- with a frightened father
- suckled by a shrinking violet of a mother
- brought up by thugs or brutes who have made it scared of people

Unless you know the puppy and its parents very well, trust the breeder. She will give you the maximum of background detail and help you to find homogeneous litters. A litter that contains one good puppy and six runts is not a good litter. To choose a good puppy from it is like playing the lottery. And everyone knows that usually, in that game, you lose.

Study of genetics taught us some time ago that if the father has one homozygous characteristic and the mother a different homozygous characteristic, a quarter of the litter will inherit from the father, a quarter from the mother and half will present intermediate characteristics, as hybrids. I have already explained the point of this. If, in the first place, the mother and father are close relatives, their offspring will resemble them closely. This is even more the case in the dog as a species, where many breeds are no longer very standardised, particularly as to character. When puppies are very alike and seem to have more in common than not, it is reasonable to assume that in time they will grow up to be like their parents.

Having said that, it is clear that no two puppies are exactly the same.

Now all you need to know is whether the parents that you are shown are genuinely the parents of your puppy…

And what about the situation where you can't see the parents, at an animal shelter or pet shop for example? All possible places where you might find the perfect little dog of your dreams. You still need to keep to the basic rules all the same; a dog that's not frightened and a good master to take on the adoption.

The breed or type

Choose the breed of your dog according to your own personal taste, but be aware that the concept of breed applies only to the outward appearance. We talk of 'type' when the dog seems to belong to a particular breed but to have no pedigree or birth certificate. For the bloodline, unless you know the puppy and its parents you are best off trusting the breeder whom you've chosen.

As long as she knows each of her puppies well, and you tell her exactly what you want in your dog, she should be able to provide what you're looking for.

The adviser

Many buyers nowadays put their trust in an experienced professional to help them find the puppy or adult dog of their dreams. For a modest sum, people prefer this solution. Good dog trainers, specialists in how dogs are used, are all suitable for this service.

Sarplaninac puppies

How do you recognise a good breeder?

By surrounding yourself with the maximum of guarantees. The best breeders are usually affiliated to a professional or to a society working for the improvement of dog breeds. These societies are re-grouped into international federations (for example the Fédération cynologique internationale, or Kennel Clubs).

These groupings create and respect set regulations. Their adherents are not back-of-a-lorry merchants. They use only good quality breeding animals and are committed to contracts that often place them under obligations beyond legal requirements. Furthermore, as they are well-established and reputable, you can always return with a complaint if you are not satisfied.

Are you buying your dog in a market or in response to a small ad by someone working on the black market? Say goodbye to your legal guarantees. Be careful – it's not always a mistake to buy your puppy in a specialist shop. Pet shops are often inspected, and a professional shopkeeper, who maintains fixed premises, has to take an interest in the pups she sells. The law ensures that the shopkeeper is responsible for certain guarantees. Serious businesspeople respect the laws, notably those which require them to tend the puppies as adult dogs, and to vaccinate and give them an official identification before sale.

Unless you have particularly good reasons to do otherwise, leave the final choice to a breeder or experienced shopkeeper.

Make it clear to her what you are looking for and leave it to her to pass on to you the puppy that she thinks will suit you best. In a couple of hours, you will never know the litter as well as she does. Furthermore, under the influence of sudden exhaustion, or because he has finished his brother's food as well as his own, the most dynamic puppy in the litter might appear temporarily to be the laziest.

Don't throw yourself at the most pitiful, nor at the puniest. The baby you adopt today will be with you for eight years, on average; use your head to cool your heart.

Don't ignore the last of the litter, either, the one still left; often it's the best at the end of the day because he's learnt to compensate for his relative weakness with charm and energy.

When you actually own this new pet, pay a visit to a good vet at once. This professional will tell you honestly straight away what condition your puppy is in. Her diagnosis will also count as an expert's testimony in case of litigation.

Behavioural tests; baloney!

Americans don't like wasting their time, nor their money. They want to harvest as quickly as possible the fruits of their efforts and, as far as they are concerned, science can and should answer all questions. So it is to them that we owe several tests, intended for use by the general public, that they reckon will show with great precision the native, inherent character of a puppy, and his future.

Having established that the electroencephalogram (EEG) of a puppy doesn't change from 49 days after birth onwards, and that this corresponds exactly to that of the adult dog, they have deduced the following:

- At 49 days old a puppy is technically an adult.
- At this age, the animal has obviously received less input than an adult. Man has not had the time to make-over or falsify its real character.
- Therefore, at 49 days old, the dice are thrown. You know what sort of animal you're dealing with. It is possible to determine

the personality of a dog by objective tests. And consequently to know what he will be like when he grows up.

All good news? No! Let's consider all this a little more carefully.

Campbell's test

Starting from these assumptions, William Campbell became famous in English-speaking countries by publishing his celebrated five-point test.

1. Put the puppy on the ground and walk backwards three metres, then crouch down, facing him and gently clap your hands.
2. Put the puppy on the ground, do a half-turn and walk away at a moment when he is looking at you.
3. Place the puppy on his back and roll him from left to right for thirty seconds.
4. Lie him on his tummy and hold him in that position for thirty seconds, forcing him all the time to keep his head turned to one side.
5. From behind, lift his tummy with two hands and hold him suspended for thirty seconds.

The person who carries out these tests should be unknown to the puppy. He should stay calm, neutral and manipulate the animal gently, in a peaceful environment. The five tests should run without a break. A second person, such as the breeder, staying well out of things, should note the results.

Volhard's Test

The most celebrated extension of Campbell's Test is called PAT, Puppy Aptitude Testing. It was created in 1979 by Wendy Volhard and many American breeders have adopted it.

1. Social attraction; the examiner kneels, sat back on his heels, three metres from the puppy, saying nothing.

2. Desire to follow; the same as Campbell's exercise No 2.
3. Reaction to constraint; for thirty seconds the examiner, kneeling, forces the puppy to stay lying on his back, looking into his eyes throughout.
4. Forgiveness; immediately after that, the examiner lifts up the puppy, positions it opposite him, at a slight angle (45°), then strokes him and gets close to his face, to see if the animal will accept being stroked and eventually amicably lick this person who a few seconds earlier dominated him in such a disagreeable manner.
5. Dominance from a height; the same as Campbell's exercise No 5.
6. Fetching an object; the examiner holds the puppy. Openly he throws a ball of paper a metre in front of him, then releases the young animal. If the puppy goes to the object and fetches it, this is considered to be a sign that he will be easy to train.
7. Sensitivity to pain; pinch lightly, then with increasing force, the skin between the joints of a front paw. If the animal is very sensitive, he will only need a light restraint in training sessions.
8. Sensitivity to noise; bang a saucepan with a metal spoon a metre behind the puppy. If he doesn't react, you can really trust him. If he runs away fast, clearly that's not good.
9. Instinct for prey; hook a piece of string onto a cloth. Holding the string, make the cloth move along the ground in front of the puppy's nose. He will show whether his nature is curious, aggressive, timid or indifferent.

In my opinion, these tests are not very convincing. They suffer from a large number of significant defects:

1. From the very first contact with this sensitive little being, the buyer, and perhaps future master, creates obstacles and sometimes even causes suffering. Instead of radiating love, he makes loud noises, dominates, observes coldly.
2. Good breeders know perfectly well how to put a gloss on many things well before the 49th day. In any case, it's their rôle to bring the maximum of experiences to their little charges right from the beginning. Besides, how would you describe a breeder who kept her puppies well away from

people for the first seven weeks of their lives and who, in so doing, turned them into morons, on the pretext that she knew what the future would bring?

3. A breeder myself, I know that births in the same litter can be spread out over more than twenty-four hours. Which puppy is aged exactly 49 days at the moment of the test?

4. Whoever has lived in frequent contact with puppies knows that a little one can present completely different behaviour according to the hour of the day, without anything to predict these changes in conduct. What then is the validity of one test?

5. It is extremely easy for the uninitiated to violate the guidelines which ensure that the test runs smoothly. The examiner must be a fine connoisseur of dogs. In which case, does he really need tests?

6. The people who follow Campbell's precepts take no account of the master's personality. Besides, any competent dog-trainer can change a dog's behaviour completely, whether during its youth or years later. A puppy can change in all kinds of ways just by growing older. Every day, my work brings me proof that there is no case beyond redemption. Why would anyone want to condemn a baby dog, shut him up in a box with no right to appeal, from the very start of his life, without any consideration of the personality and competence of his future master?

7. And, in the end, who exactly are these people in whose infallible judgement we are supposed to place our trust? Docimology, the science of notation, shows that examiners get it wrong only too often. In the French baccalauréat, the qualification taken by eighteen year olds, the same answer paper on philosophy could receive 2/20 with one examiner and 18/20 with another.

It will take a lot more than some 'electroencephalogramic' theory to convince me that Campbell-type tests are accurate, even if they are recommended by numerous so-called, self-proclaimed canine pyschologists. Nevertheless, I *am* very interested in the works of the great American and German behaviourists. They have taught me a great deal because they have honestly and accurately observed dogs. Before them, no-one had carried out such studies. They have discovered important features. However, if these are not made an integral part of practical know-how, their influence on training has little use in day-to-day life.

I will repeat this; it is better to choose a good breeder, to put your trust completely in her, and to forget tests. I sincerely believe that one glance from an experienced dog professional can weigh up the main trends in a puppy's behaviour and that life can bring about so many changes.

Siberian Husky puppy

Choosing independently

Perhaps you intend to get your puppy from a friend, a shop or a shelter. You have to choose one yourself. How do you go about it?

1. Don't go for a timid puppy or dog. Turn down one that hides in the back of his box and looks at you with a bewildered air. But you feel so sorry for him? Leave other buyers to fall for that. Don't believe that your bottomless love will make him happy. It's far more likely that he will poison your life.
2. Don't buy a biter; he's a scared dog who's gone off the rails.
3. Don't seek out the litter leader. You often hear people use this term, 'alpha dog'. Don't be misled by it. The only one dominant 'alpha' has to be you! In reality, in any one litter, dominant status is held alternately by one, then another, of

the puppies. As pity is an emotion unknown in the animal kingdom, if there really was one completely dominant, he'd kill his brothers and sisters.

4. Shun the puppy that's skinny, ill, that coughs, or that has a runny nose, or fur like an old dry feather-duster.
5. And, within these limits, if you're still hesitating between animals of good quality, let your instinct guide you.
6. And then shower him with love and kindness, this puppy who will be at your side for many years. Don't start off your relationship with the cold behaviour of a laboratory research scientist. This baby is aware of his own physical frailty. Surround him with warmth, not with science.

Official papers

During the sale, one kind of document is obligatory under common laws; the bill of sale, which must show the date of sale and delivery, the identity of the pet, its intended use and the price of the sale. If there is no charge for the pet, it is a good idea if the owner provides a certificate stating that it is free, even if this is hand-written simply on plain paper.

The identification of a pet dog is a legal requirement almost everywhere in the world.

The dog can be identified by

- either a tatoo certificate, which has the tatoo number as pre-recorded on a computer register. The letters and numbers on the roll entry (for example, RAS 357) correspond to what is written in ink or dermographic crayon in the dog's ear on inside his thigh. This certificate is provided by a vet or by a tatooist authorised by the authorities, and the tatoo number is pre-recorded on a computer register
- or the number of the electronic chip. Nowadays, the technique of identification by electronic tagging is gradually becoming the norm. An electronic chip, capable of carrying a variety of data, from its civic status to its health record, is inserted under the dog's skin. An external reader allows the chip to be read and the data recorded on the chip to be modified.

Picardy Shepherd Dog puppy

However, respected breeders have found that sometimes these chips disappear.

Either they have shifted about the dog's body or they have been expelled. How? No-one is exactly sure but the reader stays silent when presented with some dogs that have definitely been chipped in the proper way, and are not part of any illegal trade.

Veterinary matters

In most countries, the vaccination certificate is also a legal requirement. In addition, laws frequently state that the buyer can cancel the sale if the newly acquired puppy develops certain diseases. If any of these exists, the buyer has a short period of time from the day he acquires the animal, or following the pet's death, to show intention to cancel the sale, or, following the pet's death, to claim compensation.

It should be understood that these legal details can be changed on the spot by the relevant authorities, according to the national situation in a particular country and health concerns in any given place and time. Whatever the case, your vet – or the specialist adviser who can be consulted at dogmasters.com – is the best placed to give advice.

Pet Passport

Some nations have recently created a standard 'pet passport'. This document re-organises all the information regarding identification and vaccination, facilitating customs checks. As it stands at the

West Highland white terrier puppy

moment, each country has its own requirements for the entry and exit of pets. You are therefore advised to get this information from your vet or from the Embassy of the country you would like to visit.

Legal Guarantees

Don't put any faith in other documents, or in 'pedigrees', obtained from organisations other than those commonly known. Do prefer the only organisations that offer guarantees recognised by the dog world. Some people, blacklisted by the official associations because of their dubious activities, have set up federations, associations and registers with the most weird and wonderful names. Don't get taken in!

Once the transaction is concluded, the buyer has a right to a guarantee against any hidden faults in the animal. Amateur breeders often invoke clauses that limit their responsibility. They assert that, because they don't have the expertise of professionals, they can't have a proper knowledge of all the possible problems in a breed. Don't listen to them.

There is come-back against the breeder, sometimes for as long as five years following the sale. It is up to the buyer to prove that there has been a fraud (fraudulent action, trick, or conspiracy to mislead, according to civic codes), that he has been the victim of a significant error (false pedigree, dissimulation of a fact that is likely to have led to him canceling the sale...) The buyer who believes he was wronged should take the matter up with the Fraud Squad in his county or state as soon as possible, or, better still, with a good lawyer.

Pedigree dogs

A dog registered with good organisations leaves the breeder accompanied by its birth certificate. This document is only given to animals with pedigree parents. It contains all the details identifying the dog, including its ancestry going back three or four generations.

The pedigree dog will often have an individual name such as 'O'Nut Glen Tickety-Boo'. In this title, 'O'Nut Glen' is the prefix of the breeder, her distinctive brand name.

Each breed is defined by its standard, that is to say, by a detailed description that should be the perfect exemplar for that breed. For the most popular breeds there are specific breed clubs.

In the English-speaking system, the federal structure is called the Kennel Club. The judges there are experts, invited by those who organise dog shows, and chosen according to the sole criterion of reputation.

The world is therefore divided into two great families, that of the Fédération cynologique internationale and that of the Kennel Clubs. There are numerous bridges and regulations for good practice in common between the two, which allows someone to, for instance, buy a little Westie in Great Britain and obtain breeding authorization for it in France.

Bloodhound puppy

CHAPTER 3

Your dog is a person!

'My dogs have brought me happiness all my life, for the same reasons as my children'

ALAIN DELON, *L'HEBDO*, 22ND SEPTEMBER 2005

Go, tell it on the mountain. Why not! You have dreamed about it, he's spent his first weeks with the breeder and now he's here, in your home. So, these are a few common sense tips for starters, to help you live on good terms with your companion.

His first day in his new home

- Don't hold your puppy by his paws or you risk dislocating them, nor by the scruff of his neck, which is well known as the way a mother punishes the little animal. Instead, take hold of him around the chest and underneath the tummy, both hands forming a basket. Then bring him close to you as quickly as possible, where it's warm, as if you're cradling a child.
- Stress can kill a puppy and everything can stress him out; being scared on a car journey, loud voices, brusque gestures…
- Ask your vet for worming medication if you think your puppy might have parasites. We've seen 10 day old puppies die of ascaris, the most common worms affecting dogs. Modern de-wormers cause no problems of tolerance. They can be given without the need for food beforehand and with no risk of overdose.
- A normal puppy sleeps twenty hours out of twenty-four. Let him choose his own corner to curl up in for the first time,

then put his basket there, or his blanket, or, even better, his inside den, his 'crate', that is to say a box with a door, like an airport transit box. Then, when he's asleep, leave him in peace!

- The ideal surface area for a kennel is 3m², with a play area of 12m², 4m² of which is under cover. In his crate the dog will have 1m² of decking. If you put an infrared lamp 1m above him, he will never be cold. For two dogs permanently in the kennel, use the formula devised by the French National Council for the Protection of Animals; divide the dog's height in cm (taken to the shoulder bones, the 'withers') by 2.5 and allow 3m² of ground per cm. This means two huskies of 60cm would need a kennel area of 72m².

German Shepherd Dog puppy

- Bleach is the ideal cleaning product. Unfortunately it has the unwanted side-effect of encouraging dogs to urinate where bleach has been used. It is therefore better to wash and rinse soiled areas with white vinegar.
- If your puppy leaves his little droppings on the pavement, don't try to teach him the 'gutter routine' yet. Just clean up and throw away the offending mess without saying a word. If he loses control in the house, keep exactly the same calm attitude.
- Always leave fresh water available to your new friend. You can take it away after seven o' clock in the evening so he doesn't get bloated and pass the night desperate to urinate.

West Highland white terrier puppy

- Don't think you have to run to the vet if your dog has drunk a little water from a puddle that lay in his way. But watch out for the serious modern illnesses. Parvovirus in particular. These illnesses kill.
- As a matter of urgency, hide all the dangerous products which fill your house, from slug-killer to sink-unblocker.
- If your hand's clean, don't think twice about plunging it into his foodbowl and leaving it there. Your puppy has to accept anything from you without him trying to attack. And that includes you interfering with his food. However I don't do this because my pups are on full-time self-service and, besides, I think it's rude to disturb someone when he's eating!
- He doesn't need lots of space, he needs you. For choice, collect your new puppy at the beginning of a weekend or of holidays, so that you can devote your time entirely to him for the first two or three days of your life together.
- Take him out at least twice a day, four times if you can. Stay away from places where there are other dogs; they carry diseases against which your pet is not yet fully protected.
- Don't be afraid to put a jacket on him; he is still very young and vulnerable. Cold might make him ill but mockery won't!
- Buy him some basic equipment; lead, collar and a good quality long line, all well-made and comfortable.
- Use a good insecticidal collar against fleas, ticks and mites. The best ones give four months free of irritation.

- For reassurance try insurance! At the very least, read over the policy regarding your civic duty. Call your insurer to check whether any destruction caused by your dog is covered. For best cover, take out insurance for Bonzo against illness and accident.
- Don't let your children harm your puppy, even unintentionally. He could remember this abuse all of his life.
- Call the breeder if you have a problem. She knows what to make of her stock and is familiar with clients' difficulties.

Rottweiler puppy

The master's legal responsibility

You are responsible for your dog, or for one that someone has trusted you with, and that you 'use', even if he escapes from you or gets lost. You are to blame if the animal causes any damage, unless you can prove that the victim did something wrong, or that there was a major external cause, for example if a wasp had stung him just before the incident.

You can be cleared of responsibility in an instance of legitimate defence, whether on your behalf or for someone else, in a robbery, in trespass either into a property or a house, or when your dog is attacked by another animal.

All the same, it depends on what the victim has done wrong, and how serious this is, as to how responsibility for the damage is allocated.

It is therefore best to take a maximum of precautions from the outset. Far better to take insults from passers-by, 'You brute, keeping a permanent muzzle on a sweet dog like that!', rather than have to explain in front of a tribunal and in front of the family of a child bitten by your dog, why you didn't put a muzzle on this volatile animal.

Labrador puppy

It's also a good idea to put up a sign along the lines of 'Beware the dog!' at the entrance to your house or apartment.

The law does indeed allow anyone to possess an animal in a private dwelling, but it is equally clear that one person's liberty ends where another's begins. Your dog does not have the right to annoy your neighbours, notably by leaving its droppings on the pavement or with prolonged barking. Whatever the hour of day or night.

In public places, you need to pay attention to the particular regulations that apply. Generally, dogs are not allowed in shops that sell food, nor to wander freely in streets, arcades or markets. In every country there are specific constraints that you should find out about from the relevant authorities. Sometimes the managers of public buildings – such as post offices or tax offices – impose bans. It needn't be a national regulation. It all depends on local administrative decisions.

Dogs are not banned from the streets. But they should only be there if taken on leads. For certain breeds, pit-bulls and similar types for example, the law requires that they wear muzzles in some situations. This regulation is not victimization; it is to avoid the many incidents in which, by definition, it is our dogs that come off worst.

The more of a nuisance dogs create, the less the general public likes them.

There are also legal penalties for allowing dogs to roam freely, that is, leaving them unsupervised, even in a courtyard if it is open to the public. On the other hand, a well-trained dog can be hundreds of metres away from his master and still completely supervised, directed and controlled. It is defined as roaming if the animal, left to its own natural instincts, can be considered to be a dog on the loose.

Nowadays, the laws are becoming more and more restrictive regarding big dogs. The practical implications can be complex. In this area your vet can, once more, give you useful information. So can the police, so don't hesitate to call in at your nearest police station to ask for the latest laws and regulations.

Specialist insurance

Tribunals listen more and more sympathetically to people's complaints about dogs. They even uphold claims for purely psychological damages. Rather than have to pay out large sums of money, get some insurance.

Insurance can be divided into three subcategories; civic responsibility, health/surgical and risk to life or property.

Civic responsibility can be covered in two ways, either by requesting an extension of your current household policies, likely to require an extra premium to cover a guard-dog, or by taking out specific insurance such as 'insurance for the civic responsibility of dog-owners or guardians' or 'civic responsibility for guard-dogs', or even a special contract, if, for example, the animal trains for competitive sporting events.

Health/surgical insurance, the health service for dogs, is relatively expensive and not offered by all companies.

For insurance against risk to life or property, the animal is covered up to an amount determined by the owner.

We should point out one particular condition, the one offering professional assistance in case of need, useful in many situations, notably when the master is hospitalised and can't look his dog himself.

Bobtail puppy

Boarding kennels

Not everyone can, or wants to, take Bonzo on holiday. Boarding kennels then take over from the owner. We're talking here about establishments specialising in homing dogs temporarily. You might resort to one of these for all kinds of reasons, perhaps even just to take a break as the tiredness builds up from daily contact with your over-exuberant four-footed friend. Don't hesitate to find out about the kennel-owner and her staff before you take your protégé there. Remind yourself that cleanliness isn't everything; above all, your dog needs love, even more so when you're not there. Note the behaviour of the kennel inmates, check whether your dog is happy to go back to the place, and the people, on a second occasion.

You'll be asked for your vaccination record when you book your dog into the kennels. This is a wise precaution intended to protect him, and to protect his holiday neighbours.

Animal protection

Some people commit acts of cruelty and inflict ill treatment on their own dogs or on those of others. Everyday cruelty, the most common, can be seen at the start of the motorways leading to the top holiday destinations. There you will see them regularly abandoned, some tied up, some not, the dog-gadgets.

If you witness criminal acts carried out on a dog, or on any other animal, take action. Collect witness statements, write to the State Prosecutor, go to the police, and inform the various animal welfare organisations. You don't have to be the victim to file a complaint.

Nevertheless, don't be tempted to exaggerate, even a little; if you see an owner make his dog stay down by shaking a warning fist at a sign of disobedience, don't go crying 'ill-treatment'. The law also forbids defamation of character.

Increasingly, judges are being called to intervene in other matters to do with dogs. Such is the case with dogs from 'broken homes'. The divorce procedure of separation by mutual consent, although it simplifies the formalities, concerning itself only with issues of visiting and overnight rights, prevents judges from getting bogged down in matrimonial affairs. Nevertheless a legal judgement is sometimes necessary. But lawsuits make slow progress and the life of a dog is sometimes very short…

The death of a dog

'In the life of a man there are three horses. In the life of a horse, there are three dogs.' Yavan Sultan Selim Han

One day or another, your much-loved companion will close his eyes forever. Despite the pain of bereavement, you still have to shoulder your responsibilities right to the end. Once again, your vet can help you.

You have the option of burying your dog in a property belonging to you. The grave must be deep enough and covered with quicklime. It must also be in keeping with various hygiene regulations, particularly those concerning the pollution of underground water courses. In all the towns in the world, it is in the town hall that you can obtain information on what you must do. You could also call on pet cremation services.

On the death of your dog, start reading books on puppies!

And don't make the mistake of comparing the newcomer to the dear departed; on any one tree, no two leaves are identical...

Don't wallow in the gloom of endless mourning. I have never seen a master who carried on crying over the death of an old dog once the new puppy arrived. Don't forget; the dog is dead – long live the dog!

Rhodesian ridgeback

CHAPTER 4

A dog in good health

Life is in the gut

DOCTOR OF VETERINARY MEDICINE, MICHAEL KLEIN

The pointers

Attempting to train or work a sick dog is equivalent to torturing him. So you have to be able to detect a health problem as quickly as possible. Above all, common sense will tell you most things. There is a problem if

- your dog seems unhappy and doesn't get up to greet you as usual.
- he has diarrhoea or, the opposite, suffers from constipation. In the latter case his abdomen is hard to the touch.
- his urine is dark or strong-smelling.
- his eyes are dirty, covered in yellow pus.
- his nose is dry, flaky and cracked.
- he walks with his head on one side, groaning.
- the inside of his ear smells unpleasant.
- his fur is dry and comes out in clumps.
- he is itchy with red patches of eczema.
- he walks stiffly, in a jerky manner, and staggers.
- instead of devouring his food, he picks at it.

Whatever the cause, as soon as something strikes you as unusual, some detail that just doesn't seem right, consult your vet.

Frankly it is better to err on the side of over-protectiveness than by neglect. Even if he can't or doesn't want to complain, a dog suffers too when he is ill.

To get some extra information, you can always take his temperature (in his rectum, not in his mouth). This should normally stay at 38.5°C for a relaxed animal. Don't panic if the temperature is 41°C immediately after a long session of field tracking. To establish the frequency of his pulse, place two or three fingers flat, high up on his inner thigh, perpendicular to the bone. The normal rhythm is 80-120 pulses per minute, for a dog in a state of repose. This reading could as much as double during action.

The number of inhale-exhale breathing cycles per minute should be about 15, always measured during repose and not when the heat forces the dog to pant in order to cool himself down. Unlike a human or a horse, a dog doesn't sweat from his whole body. His thermal regulation system is made up of an insulating jacket, his fur, and clumps of sudiferous cells between the plantar pads of his feet. To complement these, when a dog wants to cool down quickly, he breathes quickly, mouth open. Air then passes over the tongue and cools the blood, which in turn cools down the circulation system. A dog's fur conserves the energy used by the organism to cool down.

Over time, your vet will teach you to deal with recurring health problems yourself. Some are essential, even for the hardiest beast. If, for example, your dog suffers five times a year from an outbreak of auricular catarrh (a sort of brown muck which invades the ear trumpet), you need to treat this systematically, right from the first signs of infection, with the same specific product that has already proved effective, without necessarily running to the vet. It can be extremely beneficial for training if the owner administers some simple medicines himself; the animal learns not to panic when a human hand comes close to him to open his mouth or slip him some pills.

De-wormers

The most important treatment, the one most neglected and the one that makes the most radical difference to a dog's energy, is de-worming. Worms burrow away surreptitiously.

No need for panic, these are parasites and they are not designed to kill the host that shelters them. They are contented to merely siphon off his food and therefore his energy. A thousand times I've seen dogs recover extraordinary vitality one or two days after being treated for worms. Indeed, after such a treatment, numerous little irritations often disappear as if by magic; bloated stomachs, weeping eyes, eczema... in short all these little worries, for which people seek complicated explanations, are often cleared up by a simple worming treatment.

De-wormers exist in the form of tablets, paste, powder or injections. None of them is multi-functional so will not kill roundworms and tapeworms all in one treatment. Only an analysis of the dog's stools, carried out by a medical laboratory can identify any rebellious worms and then attack them with a specific treatment. Nowadays effective de-wormers don't require withdrawal of food beforehand.

Short-haired German pointer

Vaccinations

The other regular treatment, vaccination, is sometimes compulsory.

To buy a dog, devote your time to him, give him attention and pay for the various expenses of getting him out and about, and then not to have him fully vaccinated... you might as well play Belgian roulette (the version where the six holes of the cylinder all contain live rounds!) Follow your vet's instructions to the letter and don't forget the booster jabs.

One inoculation that isn't always considered, but that seems indispensable to me, is that which protects against blood piro- plasmosis, a terrible disease caused by ticks. A dog that has suffered this for one day might never be good for anything for the rest of his life. Much like malaria, which has ruined the health of more than one European diplomat, and of millions of poor people in the third world, blood piroplasmosis has wrecked training in many an animal. It is a stealthy disease. You think it's been cured, then, without the slightest warning, there is a new crisis, the dog is at the end of his resources and he is left the mere shadow of his former self.

The fight against parasites

Even the best-kept, cleanest animal with the best home, might one day play host to ticks, fleas or mange. All of a sudden, he's scratching, biting himself until he draws blood, or rubbing him- self frenetically against any hard object. Sometimes he loses sleep over it. Or you might discover a lump as big and red as a grape at the base of one ear. A tick!

These vermin poison dogs' lives. They are easily kept at bay by insecticides. Your vet, once again, knows which particular treatment to apply to skin mites that create burrows underneath the skin, to fleas that fall onto the ground to sleep in peace each day after they've feasted on blood, or to ticks that squat in a dog's most sensitive parts.

Many people, myself included, believe in anti-parasite col- lars. These accessories, made from porous plastic, disperse an insecticide that bathes the dog in an atmosphere hostile to insects, usually for several months. They are remarkably effi- cient. However beware some of these collars, which can have a harmful effect on your dog's sense of smell. Choose one that doesn't have too overpowering an impact, and be careful to remove it when grooming or bathing your dog.

There are also products that can be sprayed over the animal's whole body, or drops of oil that spread insecticide right across the animal's skin. Your vet will be able to give you the best advice. Simply reject those products containing dangerous molecules. If you are on the Internet, you can check http://www.pesticide.org/factsheets.html

And if your dog does have a tick, the special twist-and-pull tick extractor available from your vet or chemist is great fun!

Coat and fur

Depending on the breed, grooming is either a daily requirement (Afghans) or non-existent (boxers). Everything depends on the quality of the hair. With a Briard, for instance, a good coat, dry and wavy, needs a full comb through only once a month, whereas woolly fur, a fault according to the breed standard, mats so quickly that it is essential to untangle the hair daily if you want your pet to look well-groomed.

Regardless of grooming, check your dog's coat every day. Run your hand over his body to check for any sign of ticks or skin lesions, then carefully examine his sensitive zones; eyes, nose, ears, mouth, genitals, anus and the soles of his feet.

If you have a long-haired dog, give him a full grooming session, at regular intervals (more frequently when he's shedding), in the direction the hair grows and then against it, to remove loose hair. For short-haired animals, use a brush made of natural bristles.

Nowadays there is an excellent brush that is both flexible and durable, the zoom-groom. You'll find it in the dog-baggy catalogue on dogmasters.com.

You can also remove shed hairs by passing a slightly moist hand through the dog's fur. For my part, I consider the best grooming session to be a good swim in a clean pool. Apart from the excellent muscular and mental training provided, it stimulates skin health. The only precautions that you should take are those regarding the cleanness of the water and the absence of dangerous currents. After a swimming session, there is a risk of your dog catching a chill, especially in winter. A dog that's soaked through should not stay motionless in the cold, or, even worse, in a cool breeze.

Unless your dog's covered in oil or cowpats, shampooing is not necessary. It destroys the fine coating of waterproof oil that protects the animal from damp and allows him to dry very quickly after a bath. After a shampoo, this coating takes about three weeks to recover its full strength. Several thorough brushes, followed by a good rub-down with a clean cloth, will remove even the most stubborn dirt.

In your car, a simple doormat is the best way of covering the floor. The animal can cling onto it round bends, dried mud can bed into it and disappear. Dead hairs collect there instead of floating throughout the vehicle. You remove them simply by rubbing them with a slightly moist hand. This same technique of a moist hand is remarkably effective in cleaning jumpers, carpeting or seats covered in hair.

The crate, Varikennel or Petcargo also offers an excellent way of keeping your dog in his own secure area in the car. Further details on dogmasters.com.

Which food?

'You are what you eat.' Teaching of Yi Jin, Zhou Dynasty

Make sure your pet gets enough to eat of a complete, balanced diet and he will behave appropriately and be capable of giving his best.

On the contrary, if you over-feed him, or under-feed him, or give a bottom-of-range product which leaves him deficient in lipids, in carbohydrates, in trace elements, in vitamins, then your dog will quickly become incapable of producing a sustained effort. Furthermore, he will have little resistance to illnesses and skin problems, he will suffer from bone ailments and his life will neither be happy nor long.

In the past, owners had no option but to prepare meals for their dogs. Cooking rice, shortcrust pastry, carrots, salad, all mixed with minced beef, with cheese curds, with powdered vitamins, then the dishes to wash … All this is very admirable if you have the time it takes every day. Without taking into account how quickly you can create a dietary deficiency just by missing out one important element, or by including in Bonzo's rations ingredients to which some dogs are allergic, such as bread, biscuits, or chocolate.

Nowadays, it is easier to resort to commercially prepared food.

Moist products in tins or dry meal have the advantage of providing a balanced, complete diet for a cost price within reach of every purse, and without the inconvenience of fussy preparation.

A dog does not need variety in his food. He only needs the ingredients essential to his organism. If, nevertheless, for your own moral comfort, you would rather vary his intake, you are spoilt for choice; no commercial foodstuff is dangerous. All are good. Some are excellent.

Rottweiler puppy

If you want to change brand, move gradually from one to another, to avoid diarrhoea. Be careful with dried meal. If the dog stuffs himself on them, he will be very thirsty. His stomach will swell up and there will be problems with the passage into the digestive system. Without mentioning the possibility of a twisted stomach.

Actions that save lives

Numerous dangers threaten an active dog; broken glass scattered on the ground, a pulled muscle or a heart attack are only some examples of what can affect his physical well-being.

Of course, as always when it's to do with a medical matter, the problem is likely to be fully resolved in the vet's consultation room. But the vet is not always to hand and it's a good idea to take responsibility yourself for the survival and safe, appropriate transport of your dog.

As for a human being, the primary aim of first aid for dogs is to maintain continuity of vital functions (respiration and blood circulation), to suppress any external causes of harm, to avoid aggravation of lesions and to rush to the vet – carefully nevertheless.

The ideal preparation is to follow the first aid training offered by the Red Cross or St John's Ambulance. Clearly, you will learn from this the actions that save human lives, but, in just exchange for the atrocious vivisection that destroys dogs' lives to tend humans', these actions could also save that of your dog.

Artificial respiration mouth-to-muzzle is exactly the same as mouth-to-mouth; pressure on an artery stops a haemorrhage just as efficiently for a dog as for a human being; and cardiac massage works with the same efficiency for a dog as for us.

There are six categories of 'critical emergencies'; cardiac arrest, suffocation, poisoning, a twisted stomach, heat-stroke and haemorrhage.

Suffocation and cardiac arrest

Learn 'Heimlich's Manoeuvre'. Check the mouth and back throat of the dog. Remove any foreign bodies that you find there. Then put your hands on the sides of the animal's thoracic cage, a little in front of its last ribs, the ones said to be floating, and give a hard squeeze, bringing your hands together. This first movement of exhalation ejects any foreign body, moving it gradually into the victim's mouth.

Move your hands apart and then repeat the squeezing action, in a movement alternating every four seconds (fifteen movements per minute). When you feel normal breathing return, follow its rhythm.

In the case of a dog that has just been pulled out of the water, put the animal on a slight slope, head lower than body, so that water can run out of the throat and lungs. An advantage of Heimlich's Manoeuvre is that it allows artificial respiration and cardiac massage simultaneously.

Poisoning

This is likely to be a spectacular incident; the dog is slobbering and can't control nerves or muscles. His eyes are rolling upwards.

Unfortunately, the appropriate actions have to be specific. It is essential to know the particular product that the dog has swallowed. Then follow absolutely minutely the instructions on the packaging.

In this area, prevention is better than improvisation; if, one day, you introduce to your household a product that needs an injection of Vitamin K as an antidote to its accidental ingestion, then stock up on Vitamin K!

A twisted stomach (bloat)

This is the most crucial veterinary emergency, the one incident that requires immediate intervention by the dog's master and then by the vet. Twisted stomach tends to happen to active dogs, and to those which sometimes stuff themselves, so we will consider these in particular.

A dog's stomach is a bit like a soldier's haversack; it hangs from two tubes, by which food comes and goes. For reasons that

Appenzell Mountain Dog

are still not really understood – type of food, rapid movement, influence of the moon – this haversack sometimes doubles up on itself. In so doing, it seals up both the entrance to and the exit from the stomach. This means that the gas produced by fermenting food can't escape. The dog's stomach swells up like a balloon. The poor animal can't breathe because his lungs are so compressed. He dies slowly, in appalling torments.

There is only thing to be done, on condition that you have the courage, and bearing in mind that the survival of the dog has this price; open the stomach as soon as possible using a clean knife blade, three centimetres long, make sure the slit stays open and ensure this by inserting a tube or similar object. There is hardly any blood as the abdomen is lined with white muscle. You must then find a vet as quickly as possible and ask for immediate intervention.

To avoid this situation

- don't ask for major exertions from your dog just after he's been eating or drinking
- don't let him drink freely after sustained exercise. A few mouthfuls suffice. It's better for you to let your dog be thirsty for an hour than to risk losing him with a twisted stomach. Be careful if his breathing doesn't calm down, especially if the weather is hot, and if you suspect that panting is not cooling him down enough. Watch out for heat-stroke.
- don't let your dog gorge himself. A stomach that is distended from one moment to the next is more likely to double up on itself. Don't forget that, in the wild, the wolf, like our dog, is capable of ingesting up to twelve kilos of meat in one go.

One day I had to induce vomiting in a German Shepherd Dog on its return from a raid into the countryside. It regurgitated the entire contents of my neighbour's dustbin; two complete turkey carcasses including feet and feathers, plus coffee dregs, melon seeds, pieces of nappies, orange peel, and the aluminium foil lids from yoghurt pots.

This greedy creature returned home by bounding over wire fencing 1m 20cm high, without so much as touching it. It was my own dog, Pacha. And he died at 4 years old from a twisted stomach, all because a vet didn't consider this complaint to be an urgent matter.

The active dog lives more dangerously than his fellows who lounge around on cushions or in a kennel twenty-four hours a day. It is therefore up to the master to make sure that the risks taken by the animal stay at an acceptable level.

There is no such thing as an intelligent accident. In the last analysis, it is always the master who is responsible when his dog has an accident.

Heat-stroke

Immerse your dog completely in cold water if you can. Hose him down for ten minutes, especially under his stomach where there is no fur. If possible, rub ice cubes over his stomach, his forehead, the back of his neck, and his tongue. Try your hardest to cool him down as much as possible. And, at the same time, call the vet.

Haemorrhage

Learn, by asking advice from your vet, how to use a pressure point, how to put on a bandage, how to apply a tourniquet.

In conclusion, for all health problems, never hesitate to consult your vet.

To choose your vet, get some information from the breeders who live near you. Profit from the selection process that they've already undertaken themselves, often following costly experiences. They know who the best in their field are. Don't go near the vet who finds a thousand problems in a perfectly healthy puppy which has only just come to live with you; even in the land of the dogs, Doctor Knock has his followers.

Morphology

You can give your dog basic training, or even progress to higher levels of obedience, without knowing the correct terms for parts of your dog's anatomy. However, using exact vocabulary shows that you are serious in your good intentions.

Physical characteristics vary enormously from one breed to another; the length, colour and texture of his hair, the shape and colour of his eyes, the set of his ears, of his tail and his dew-claws, are to a large extent the external signs of his breed identity.

We measure size with a rule that starts on the ground and rises vertically to the withers; this is a point on the back under the highest point between the scapula.

The rule also serves to measure the animal's length, which is taken from the point in front of the breast (the anterior point of the front sternum) to the back of the thigh (the point of the ischion).

One last word on morphology; unless you are the happy owner of a 57 varities-mongrel, you can only enrich your knowledge by studying the standard of your chosen breed. Each breed club has established one and even if some of the terms seem bizarre, along the lines of 'the ribs should be neither rounded nor flat', you can still learn a lot that's very interesting.

The lost dog

Morphology offers one useful aspect; a description that gives you the maximum chance of recovering your dog if he gets lost. I can't over-emphasise the importance of either tattooing, whether in the ear or in the inside of the thigh, or identification by electronic chip. Take photos, too. And if your dog has strayed off, don't lose hope. Put up posters all round the area where the dog went missing, put ads in the newspapers and offer a reward.

Free veterinary advice

If you have a question concerning the health of your dog, you can consult a veterinary surgeon, free, on dogmasters.com

CHAPTER 5

The mental mechanisms of the dog

'A dog hit by a stone tries to bite the stone not the person who threw it,'

MARCUS PACUVIUS

All living beings communicate. We distinguish intra-species communication, which, as its name indicates, takes place between members of the same species, and extra-species communication, from one species to another, as between humans and dogs.

A thousand anecdotes testify that a dog understands very well what his master tells him and that he also knows exactly how to make himself understood. For my part, I say that the dog is the non-verbal king. Remarkably intelligent, he brings to light our tiniest gesture. The human being who concentrates on words forgets to watch over his body language. Specialists in communication have proved it; our behaviour often speaks more powerfully than our words, particularly where our feelings and our state of mind are concerned.

Beside us lives our closest observer, who tries his best day after day to decode our gestures. He learns to read us once and for all. He puts a lot of time into this, as well as a remarkable flexibility and uses an extraordinary tool of which we are almost totally ignorant, despite advanced research; his uncanny sense of smell.

Perhaps he uses sensors of which we have not yet identified? On his muzzle he has long, fine whiskers, just like a cat's. If nature continues to endow Rover with these 'antennae' there must be a reason. But what? It's a mystery.

Poodles that find that their muzzles have been shaved, or as good as, by the pet groomer, have no whiskers and yet they don't lose their sense of balance, as some jokers like to suggest. They don't even knock, however lightly, against furniture in their path. So what special aspect of touch is provided by these long, hard hairs?

And what if these hairs are effectively antennae, able to receive the alpha, beta and gamma radio waves emitted unintentionally by all living creatures, the master most of all?

And what if the dog is capable of reading human minds, especially when these are under the influence of strong emotions?

And what if, once more, the dog is superior to human beings in the field of communication?

As for me, I've made up my mind; I firmly believe that dogs' and cats' whiskers are radio antennae. The experts are busy carrying out their investigations. Perhaps one day they'll confirm this theory of whisker-radar!

Meanwhile, you should be aware that some of your gestures, whether deliberate or not, give your dog information. So what then is the language of the dog? How best do you exploit to your own advantage this keen sense of observation possessed by your best friend?

Unintentional messages

Observe your own mannerisms. Do you complement your commands with certain gestures? Are these gestures identical from one day to the next, such as pointing a finger at the ground when you want the dog to come to your side? Have you set up a routine when you intend to go out? Such as always checking the clock twice in a row, just before going for a walk, instead of the once for when you intend staying at home. Your dog is the one who can easily discern all this.

If necessary, a competent trainer can help you detect your superfluous mannerisms. In fact, a trainer at competition level is highly skilled; judges give an automatic penalty of zero marks for a handler making the slightest gesture that could be considered to be a subtle signal to the dog. This means that, during the exercise of walking to heel, if the master has the misfortune to sniffle because of the cold, he loses all his points. You can understand why, burnt once, trainers quickly learn to avoid any uncontrolled movements.

On the contrary, at home, Mr Everyman spends his time sending unintentional messages, with no idea he's doing so. Everyone knows the going-for-a-walk syndrome; the dog goes crazy with excitement at almost the moment the master first decides, in his own head, that he might go for a walk. How does the animal succeed in reading a man's thoughts in this way? It's a mystery. Perhaps, when he decides to go for a walk, the master opens his eyes a little more widely than usual, or gives off a particular sweat, that fills the room with its characteristic smell?

There is always a realm of the inexplicable. And just as well, many dog-lovers would add, for in what is unknown, rests a large part of the attraction of dogs for men. This is probably the reason that dogs are indispensable to us.

The language of the dog

All breeders know that the dog has his own spoken language, that his mother probably told her little ones 'Grrrrr!' or 'Woof' meaning 'Stop chewing on my teats or look out, you!' and 'Push a bit harder!' But, if the dog has a somewhat limited vocal scale, he wins paws down with an infinite repertoire of mimes, mannerisms and action sequences.

The way he looks at you gives all kinds of information. By turns attentive, sleepy, sparkling or menacing, his eyes reflect the mood of the moment. Experts have identified a whole range of mannerisms and changes in physionomy. His ears, his forehead, his tail and paws take up different set positions depending on the dominant emotions or those arising.

Through the mediation of researchers, just as from personal experience, you can learn what an animal's mannerisms mean. It remains only to make the most of these discoveries. Trainers at competition level, just like ordinary owners who are very close to their dogs, know that with a little dog sense and perseverance it is possible to refine secret signals that are perceived and understood only by their students.

Body language

You have the right to double up on commands with gestures. In everyday life, doubled commands, tripled even, are not penalised in the way they are in competitions. And it is entirely in your interest to do this. When you command, 'Down!' for example, crouch down in front of the dog and tap the ground between his front paws. The whole movement reinforces the impact of each element; this is the principle of cumulative stimuli.

English Cocker Spaniel

To double up on a command, you should in general play on two factors essential to man-dog communication; tone of voice and body language. The dog, *a priori*, does not understand the words in themselves. Try a little experiment. Sing the word, 'Down' instead of speaking it normally; the dog won't move. What he senses is the intonation of your voice. Here again, you can put this to the test. Recall your dog with the words, 'Free beer!' using the same tone and with the same enthusiasm as 'Come here!'. There is every chance your dog will arrive on the trot. But only if he usually obeys the recall order, of course!

Body language is very effective if you want to send a message to your dog. Communication experts have analysed the rules that govern the language we all use without really being aware of it.

- Establish eye contact. This is a bit tricky because, by their nature, animals do not look into each other's eyes. This is for one essential reason; a look reveals the fear felt by one animal in the face of another of its species and gives away the exact moment that the less confident of the two is about to launch into a defensive attack.

  However, if eye contact is not customary between animals, it can take place between man and dog. For centuries, the latter has chosen to live amongst men. He trusts men and knows that the occasions on which a man, growling and biting, will attack him, are rare indeed! Therefore, if you can manage to catch the animal's eye, you can send him the gist of your message in a flash; whether you are contented, angry or determined that he will obey you.

- Stay confident. Through a well-balanced attitude you can literally be a source of serenity, empowering your dog. Your pet is equally sensible to a lack of composure; if you are wound up, he will get wound up too, and much more quickly. Then nothing can be done. On the other hand, a relaxed manner can re-establish a calm atmosphere; shoulders neither raised nor dropped back, arms open but not too widely, fingers stretched out, legs crossed when you're sitting down, all these choices of posture give a beneficial impression of ease.

- Suit your facial expression to the message you want to put over; smile when you recall your dog, widen your eyes when you're not pleased, etc

- Control your hands. No hyperactivity. For the dog, the master is, at the same time, kindness and caresses, the pleasure of food and the constraint of the lead. Everything is delivered by the hand. It is to this that the dog pays constant attention.

- Move about calmly. The human body, enormous in the eyes of the biggest hound, has an inherent authority in itself, just by being upright. This advantage is reinforced if the master uses it as part of benevolent firmness. You have never seen someone in a position of power, a queen or President of the Republic or a king, run feverishly from one place to another. Even in moments of crisis, such people walk, calmly.

The master who leaps around all the time like a kid-goat forces a timid dog to be extra-submissive and an aggressive dog to defend himself before being attacked.

Evidently these few rules of behaviour aren't enough to guarantee perfect control over your four-footed companion. But by observing them, you will work in a favourable atmosphere. Certainly, nothing is easy in this search for self-control. Let the man who has never been angry, who has never lost his cool, throw the first stone at others!

The three basic urges

Your favourite companion is not spiritually motivated. He does not believe in a metaphysical god, with unselfish notions of charity and altruism, and he has no faith in the essential goodness of beings. In essence, he reacts to three basic urges:-

- the sexual urge (towards reproduction)
- survival instinct (to find food and to defend himself)
- and pack instinct.

For the master, the two first impulses are difficult to control. You can't always lay your hand on a female in heat to attract a dog that doesn't want to come back when he's called, and for her part, a female has no interest in that whole ball-game except when she's on heat.

As regards what's needed for survival, it quickly becomes obvious that this blinds an animal in its brutality. It's better to organise things so that the dog doesn't have to consider survival at all, by giving him a healthy, balanced diet in sufficient quantities, and by personally protecting him in his early youth, after having made sure in the first place that you haven't acquired a paranoid dog that panics at the tiniest noise. In this way, you will allow your dog to develop a stable personality, and not to imagine threats everywhere.

So let's accept that your dog is not overwhelmed with sexual urges, nor by the fear of imminent death. You should therefore work on the third lever, the one that stays permanently active;

the need to live as part of a pack, in a well-established hierarchical order.

The essential characteristic of the dog rests in its perpetual desire to climb as high as possible in the social ladder. If he were a man, you'd say he is ambitious. Unless he is equipped with a particularly submissive character or you have made it clear to him from the start that there's no way he can rise above humans, your dog is going to try all his life to become leader of the pack in which he lives, your human family as it happens.

How often have I met these four-footed domestic tyrants in a reign of terror – it's not too strong a word – over Mr, Mrs and the children. And over the maid, if there is one.

Nature continues to abhor a vacuum. You can be sure that if, through misunderstood kindness and gentleness, you allow your dog to win and take the upper hand – even just a little bit – you are opening your door to the devil! It's not inevitable that he'll enter but your door is open to him.

Let's take an example. Your 7 month puppy is snuggled up under the table. You call him sweetly so you can give him a cuddle because you feel yourself in need of some affection. Your little four-footed companion turns a deaf ear. So you insist, perhaps raising your voice a little. You reach out to him and try to grab his collar so you can draw him towards you. Half-asleep, he makes vaguely grouchy noises, as if he's telling you, 'Leave me alone, you can see I'm sleeping – slow the pace down for goodness sake!' If, at that precise moment, you beat a retreat instead of firmly demanding that he gets up and comes to you, you risk being bitten one day. By these little personal defeats – little in your eyes perhaps but often repeated – you reinforce the dog's belief that he is the stronger. Sooner or later, and more likely sooner, you will be bitten. Members of your family too because, one day, your dog will decide to cross the line and risk using his teeth, just to see if this technique works equally well.

Small indulgences carry the seeds of tragic consequences. To give way in front of your dog is to condemn him to death because, when he one day bites someone, you will be asked to have him put to sleep.

It only remains to say that, often, well-meaning owners come to see me and ask, 'OK, we don't know how to go about it, it's obvious we've completely messed up but we're determined to change things from now on. What should we do?'

I always reply that they have to establish or re-establish, their position as leader of the pack. It is enough to put in place some simple structures. The first is to decide wholeheartedly that you are going to be the dog's master. Without this determination the battle is lost before it starts because, instantly, by using its secret receptors, the dog understands that his master or mistress is just a paper tiger, good for nothing but raising his or her voice to seem in authority – and the key word is 'seem'.

Basset Hound

It is then necessary to decide that, from now on, nothing is for free. The dog comes begging to be stroked? There should be nothing before it's earned, for example before he's gone down on command. He wants you to throw his ball? Before throwing it for him, make him do something for you. For example, order him to 'Go by the door!' and wait till he obeys.

Believe me, this way of behaving will save you having to get heavy later on. This technique is all the better in calling for no brutality. Quite simply, it teaches your dog not to give you orders.

How to raise your dog

What is there to say about this daft, supposedly modern attitude of parents who are opposed to any sanctions, and whose children today are lost in drugs or alcohol, incapable of making any effort or of generosity to anyone else!

A dog's master, like any parent conscious of his duties, should have the courage to accept being hated at times by the animal, during the stage of apprenticeship. This takes nothing away from a loving relationship, quite the opposite. For education is an asymetric art in which the master must, fairly, with moderation, impose his will on the student who is, for the moment, the weaker of the two. He possesses certain knowledge and he has to transmit this in the best way possible to raise his dog, by, for instance, setting the example of a personality full of virtues, of moral force, a worthy role model. It is no coincidence that both 'raise' and 'bring up' literally mean to add physical height.

In practice, do you think a bitch hesitates to cuff her puppies when she judges it to be useful?

Androcles and the lion

Above all, don't make the mistake of taking for solid currency the glittering myth of Androcles and the lion. It was the erudite Roman, Aulus Gellus, who narrated the story, in the 2nd century AD, at a time when anti-Christian repression was at its height.

Out walking one day, Androcles, the slave, came across a lion sobbing with pain and pulled a thorn out of its paw. Some time later, he was thrown into the arena because he had become a Christian. He found himself facing the same lion that he had helped, and so he was not devoured. In this way, the beast paid his debt of gratitude.

This charming story has made the tears run in torrents. Over time, the myth of Androcles has embedded itself in modern thinking. We like to give human attributes to animals. We therefore believe, without question, that dogs can show gratitude, an acknowledgement. Most of the time it is nothing of the kind.

Far be it from me to ruin a charming legend and allege that a dog never thanks its master in it own way. But, for a long time, I have had to deconstruct the mechanisms that lead to incidents, and I know all too well that hell is paved with good intentions.

The myth of Androcles and the lion has misled, is misleading and will mislead thousands of animal-owners. On the premise that he feeds his dog well, strokes him now and again, shares his house with him, Mr Everyman thinks that he has done his duty. He imagines that, like the lion on the arena, his dog will remember all this generosity. The truth is quite the reverse.

Pyrenean Sheepdog

Remember that the dog understands all your actions through the distorting mirror of the hierarchy. As I said at the beginning of the chapter; he reacts as a creature governed by a formidable pack instinct. Be his helper, his protector, his cook, whatever you want, but remain leader of the pack.

Let's take up again the case of Mr Everyman, dominated by his dog:-

- The animal receives his food-bowl. He thinks, 'Ah. My servant has brought me something to eat.'
- The beloved doggie gets stroked. He analyses this, 'Ah. my servant is once more showing an appropriate act of submission towards me.'
- The animal climbs on the bed, where he spreads out and stretches, 'Ah. It's nice to come back to my own place after a satisfying day. But am I dreaming or what! My servant wants me to get down? I'll give a good old growl to bring him back to more respectful behaviour. If that doesn't work, I might show him my fangs, or even put them to use!'

To take care of your dog, with love, with intelligence, is one of the pleasures of life. But to rely on some gratitude in his heart or mind is to commit the cardinal sin of anthropomorphism.

Anthropomorphism

A dog is not a man. It functions as a domesticated wolf. Except with regard to a true pit-bull, this holds true for every dog, whatever its size, its background or its character.

Without meaning to, and most often without realising it, man behaves as a servant in the eyes of his dog. And if, one day, the dog commits the sin of losing his temper, or even biting, the man stupidly mutters comments along the lines of, 'I don't understand. Until now he has always been so sweet, so friendly!'

Yes, sweet and friendly, like a despot, good with his subjects because they feed and look after him, but who doesn't hesitate to whip them until blood flows on a day when they annoy him.

The dog must never, at any price, be allowed to think, 'What a good boss I am!'

Rather than risk reaching that point, it's better to behave inconsistently, be moody and prone to unpredictable irritation. This way the dog will always be slightly on the defensive. Slightly, just a little on the defensive, just enough to forbid him taking over pack leadership, without breaking his spirit and personality.

Restraints

Only a salesman will assert that you can educate dogs without using restraints. The great trainers, those who prove in top competitions that they know their profession, and the most knowledgeable experts, recognise the fact that it is impossible to get a dog to obey without using any restraints. Avoid those who assert the contrary; they are lying to you. It only remains to say that if restraint proves necessary, it should not be abused nor become habitual.

I will repeat this again; always keep restraint to the lowest possible level. Return as soon as you can to minimal restraint. You have the right to use one reprimand for ten thousand caresses!

Scottish terrier

Be leader of the pack with a cool head

Save your strength. There is no need to shout or hit to become leader of the pack. On the contrary; bad temper is a short-term-madness and a dog isn't obedient to it. To make your dog obey you, to dominate him, it is better to use the one organ that really does place you higher than animals; your brain. The Americans have an excellent saying, 'Be smarter than your dog.' If your dog is beaten on the intellectual plane, if he admits that you are smarter, he will respect you. Don't rely too much on your physical strength; he has far more resources than you do.

The three best techniques that man has at his disposal to establish his dominance over his dog, in all kindness are to 'raise him, roll him and pin him down'.

Raise him

Lift up your dog by seizing hold of his withers like a mother does with her little ones. Be careful that his paws don't touch anything. Watch out that they're not pressed against you either.

Remember the legend of Anteus, the monster brought down by Hercules. Anteus, like your dog, regained its strength each time it touched the earth but lost its power when its feet left the ground. Be careful as some dogs hate being lifted. They struggle like the very devil. It is absolutely essential that you don't lose this confrontation. Organise yourself so that you will win, if need be using a muzzle, to give you total confidence in yourself.

Roll him

Get your dog to lie down, then roll him onto his back, all four feet in the air so that they no longer touch the ground. This reversal reproduces the pose of submission adopted by the loser after a scrap; the defeated dog offers his throat and stomach to the winner, as if to say, 'Go on then, you can kill me, I'm not defending myself against you any more.'

You will have won, the day your dog, as soon as you roll him on his side, presents his stomach and throat to you.

Pin him down

With your dog lying on his back or his side, lean over in front of him, and gently massage all of his body. In this way, you are reproducing the image of the conqueror who chews at his defeated adversary and pins him to the ground to make it very clear who's boss.

In these ways, taking multiple occasions to establish and reinforce your position as leader, you are impacting at one and the same time on the conscious and subconscious of your canine companion. Given the role of your lieutenant and knowing his own place in a clearly defined hierarchical order, your dog can now become the best of officers.

Trust

As a general rule, the dog that doesn't complain and that looks at his master with trusting eyes at the very moment the vet is sticking a needle into him for vaccinations, is not saying, 'I have such a good master. He is really looking after my future health, thanks to this little jab that will protect me from now on against contagious diseases.' Rather more prosaically, he's saying, 'OK, he's giving me more grief again, this person, but I have learned not to lose my temper and bite at the slightest reason, and to stay down when I'm given the command. So, I'll just stay cool, because my master is asking me to be sensible. And I know that my master or that man in green will really tell me off if I snap to defend myself...'

At best, he'll add, 'Pouf, let's trust this man I spend my days with. He's not the sort of brute who tortures me for pleasure. His ways are mysterious. He probably has a good reason for inflicting this pain on me.'

The trust that you read in the eyes of your dog, is the confidence he has in himself, but equally, as in a mirror reflecting another mirror, it's your own self-confidence!

Don't forget,' Like master, like dog!'

A dog's character

Genetically, the dog is a wolf. Evolution of the canine species has created the breeds we know today, from the Chihuahua to the mastiff, but it hasn't changed its character in any fundamental way. Whether we are ready to admit it or not, a sweet doggie is a wolf in arrested infancy.

A puppy comes into the world with certain particular tendencies. Like his ancestor, he is capable of learning at a very rapid rate what he is told by his 'inner schoolteacher', that is to say his whole collection of instincts.

We've seen that he never forgets what he learned during the first fourteen weeks of his existence. What is less well known is that, the more experiences the puppy stores up during this period of 'canine kindergarten', the more quickly he assimilates new information. He learns to learn. The more rapidly he establishes good reactions and good attitudes, in the face of setbacks thrown at him by Life, the more likely he is to respond appropriately to new situations.

Moreover, as he quickly adapts to the life he leads, you could say that a dog is, to a great extent, the product of his environment.

A dog's behaviour is not, however, solely dependent on the impact of the environment. With dogs, as with humans for that matter, it is more a question of a dynamic phenomenon, compromise and interaction between the individual (with his own characteristics) and the environment. One animal might run away when he hears a car coming while his litter-brother comes out howling to snap at the tyres and yet the two have always lived together and have much the same stock of experiences.

This dialogue between the individual and his world, this creation of a definitive code of behaviour, corresponds to a spiral of learning. The design of this spiral shows how the little wolf-dog and his environment react in relation to each other but also how the two partners, if we can describe them that way, end up intermingled. At the end of the journey, it is impossible to distinguish with certainty cause and effect in the development of character.

Pyrenean Mountain Dog

It is for this reason that German ethologists, after Konrad Lorenz – the first to have spoken of the way the environment imprints on the mental system of a young animal – prefer the term 'behavioural mix' to the word 'character'. Professor Seiferle gives the following full definition of 'character'; 'It is the combination of tendancies, characteristics, plus mental and physical aptitudes, both innate and acquired, which determine, shape and govern the behaviour of the dog within its environment.'

Mental adaptability and intelligence grow over time, on condition that life is varied and demanding enough without crossing the threshold of homeostasis, in other words the level at which an animal is so panic-stricken that the sole effect is to block any beneficial process of learning.

For instance, one puppy is not afraid when the fridge door bangs shut right beside him but continues his exploration of the kitchen, while another, panic-stricken by the same event, hides under the staircase for hours before daring to poke out his nose.

The rôle of the master is therefore to do his best to shape the character of his companion. The principle is twofold; you should offer your pet as many new situations as possible and you should watch over him to make sure he comes through without fear or danger.

Let's not harbour any rosy dreams; we can't change all of a dog's behaviour. But with love and, of course, with the techniques, we can improve on everything.

The five senses

Right from the start, we have often repeated that the dog is a wolf. To put it more simply, he possesses the same capacity to adapt to his environment and the same intelligence.

But what is this wolf like? How does he function? What are his strengths and weaknesses? To answer these vast questions, let's first investigate his sensory characteristics; smell, hearing, sight, touch, taste and then the instincts that drive him.

Smell

You will understand nothing about a dog until you accept that he is a nose on four legs. When you reach a certain level in the art of training dogs, you confront this incontestable fact; the biggest physical difference between man and dog rests in their respective capacities to use the sense of smell.

Man is almost 'nose-blind'. His 5 million olfactory cells are all found in a surface of a few square centimetres. While the 220 million olfactory cells of a German Shepherd Dog are shared out along a concertina of skin tissue, which, if it was completely unfolded, would completely cover the dog's whole body! In 1955, the German expert Neuhaus established that the sensitivity of the canine nose is between one hundred thousand and one hundred million times more developed than that of the human nose.

Another researcher, Vitas Droscher, carried out an enlightening experiment. One gramme of butyric acid, a substance that smells of rancid butter, contains 7 thousand billion billion molecules. A man is capable of sensing the presence of one gramme of butyric acid in a building of six stories. With one degree more of dilution, the man ceases to detect the rancid butter but the dog can still do so. The dog can still pick out the smell when the gramme of acid is spread out in a volume of 400square km by 100m high!

The dog also possesses extraordinary powers of discrimination. He knows how to distinguish between two smells that are very closely related.

We can compare this capacity to discriminate with what we ourselves are capable of on the visual plane. We have the ability to detect miniscule differences in shade between closely related colours. Experts, specially trained, can go to amazing lengths in visual discrimination. For example, the Inuits use a hundred different terms to describe the different colours of snow. In the domain of smell, the dog seems even more talented.

Multiple examples prove it. The bloodhound can find people who have been lost for as long as eight days; the labrador can detect a packet of cocaine even disguised by strong ammoniac smells; the little Breton spaniel can pick up the smell of a hare from several hundred metres. Sometimes, a dog will stop dead when there is nothing to be seen, and show signs of being very excited, to the point where we brave people imagine and comment that he has 'seen a ghost.' In reality, the wind has brought him an appetising waft, which has put the animal in turmoil but has completely bypassed the man, un-noticed.

Certain breeds are better known than others for what trainers call 'a nose.' But you can also come across a 'great nose' in a breed not renowned for this characteristic. One such was Ubac, a little Pyrenean Shepherd and French Champion of search and rescue in 1987.

The nose works as a specialised sensor, capable of detecting and identifying one smell among thousands of others. There are people nowadays who affirm that the muzzle contains cells capable of detecting infra-red rays, as in snakes that can locate their prey by the heat given off.

If you want to surprise your four-footed student at any

moment, you therefore have to be doubly, no, triply or even quadruply, cautious. When, for instance, you want to sneak up on him unawares, remember that his sense of smell will give him warning as well as his infra-red detectors.

He might hear you too.

Hearing

After smell, this is his second strength. Any owner knows how, with great discernment, the canine ear can perceive the slightest noise. Everyone knows the story of a dog that can pick out the particular noise made by his master even in the midst of the densest traffic.

This discrimination seems almost magical when, for example, the dog goes mad with excitement five minutes before the arrival of a familiar visitor who only comes two or three times each month.

The dog can detect more sounds than a human being.

We know that sounds are born from vibrations and also travel by vibrations, which move a bit like waves do when you drop a pebble in a pool.

As they leave source of the noise, the waves are more or less closely spaced, and higher or lower. The variation in how high the waves are (the modulation of amplitude or AM) or the distance between peaks (modulation of frequency or FM) determines the modification of sounds. A very high sound comes from a very rapid vibration, 40,000 hertz for example, or 40,000 vibrations, 40,000 waves, per second. A bass note corresponds to a lower frequency, 8,000 hertz for example.

The dog continues to hear infra-sounds, that is to say vibrations at frequencies below the audible threshold, and ultrasounds, the same thing but above the upper threshold, while the human ear has given up much earlier.

At the beginning of the twentieth century, German experts Katz and Engelmann carried out a revealing experiment. While volunteers with very good hearing could discern the sound of material being crumpled 6 metres away, a German Shepherd Dog could hear it from 25 metres!

Sounds outside the audible range, barest hints of sounds – a dog's ear detects all of these with no problem. But this ability to capture infinitesimal sounds is doubled by an amazing capacity to discriminate, to distinguish between sounds.

The Austrian expert von Frisch reports an experiment in which he had put a collie at the centre of a collection of loud-speakers placed in a circle. One researcher switched on one loud-speaker. The dog was supposed to rush at that one. He would find a slice of sausage there as a reward. If he got the wrong loud-speaker, no sausage! With up to sixty loud-speakers, the dog made not one single mistake; he could determine with absolute precision which loud-speaker produced the 'sausage-noise'. As a comparison, von Frisch asked six human guinea-pigs to take the dog's place. From only seventeen loud-speakers, none of them could localise the source of the noise with any certainty.

Between the hearing of a man and that of a dog, there are certainly less differences than between their respective senses of smell. Yet, here again, a dog can leave a man behind at the starting blocks. During this period of training, then right through your dog's life, you should take care not to get left behind. A dog hears everything and has an excellent audio-memory.

On this subject, Captain Max von Stephanitz, the godfather of the German Shepherd Dog relates an astonishing experience. In 1926 he had been training the bitch Daga von Blasienberg at home for several months. Then he returned her to her owner. One day, during the same year, at a competition in the town of Breslau, Stephanitz was invited to judge and to make the opening speech. Accompanied by her master, who was attending as a competitor in the event, Daga was there, at the back of an immense hall, which was crammed full by the crowd.

She stood up, quivering, from the very first words by the speaker. Right until the end of the speech, she stayed perched on a chair, her body stretched towards the stage from where Stephanitz was speaking, obviously without a microphone. The dog had recognised the voice of her second master straight away. And he, clearly, had known how to win her heart...

We should learn to respect this marvelous tool. The noises of modern life attack the dog's sensitive ear every day. This does not cope with loud noises easily. Avoid car radios that blare in the

Bulldog

ears of your poor little dog, lying there in the car, at the foot of the passenger seat. For the animal it is a veritable torture. Imagine yourself having to wear a walkman for three hours with the volume turned up to its limit.

It is well known that men in artillery regiments often suffer from early deafness due to the detonation of their guns, and that rock musicians very quickly lose whole sections of their hearing range from constantly performing among high decibels.

Moreover, the ear suffers several little problems. The most frequent are inflammations caused by spikelets, by parasites like mange or by auricular catarrh.

Regular use of a disinfectant solves these problems but you must go to the vet if the condition persists. Luckily, the dog knows perfectly well when there's something wrong with his ear; he tilts his head on one side, shakes it, scratches at it, either a little or a lot, and moans.

Sight

It's a fact that dogs don't see well. It's probably because of this that they put their sense of smell and hearing to such good use, as a kind of alternative, or compensation.

In the film 'Wolfen[1]' we can discover one aspect of canine vision as interpreted by the experts. The dog sees colours vaguely, more in sepia tones. He can detect infra-red rays but objects appear deformed to him, a bit like photographs taken with a fish-eye lens.

He can see moving objects well. On the other hand he manifests difficulties in identifying precisely objects or creatures that are static. This is where has the advantage. Except in one detail; the dog sees much better than man in the dark.

Sometimes you'll see a dog's eyes take on a fluorescent tint, purplish-red or bright green. This phenomenon is due to a thin film, phosphorescent in appearance, that covers the back of the eye and amplifies the tiniest amount of light. At night, a dog's iris is reduced to a very thin ring. The whole area is occupied by the pupil, which dilates widely as if to suck in the smallest luminosity.

Some animals, such as the cat, can see equally well at night as during the day. their eyes shine like catadioptric reflectors in our vehicle headlights. But it's the wolf that leaves the most striking impression on those who come across one at night. Its eyes, like torches, seem on fire like burning coals.

Its direct descendant, our dog, knows how to move in the dark without bumping into furniture or trees in the forest. The numerous cells in the retinal rod that lines the back of the eye are what give him this extraordinary night vision. However, sensitive only to white light, they do not allow him to interpret colours accurately.

If his vision is not as impressive as his hearing or sense of smell, especially from a distance, it still deserves the greatest care.

We're not talking here of amaurosis, of cataracts or progressive atrophy of the retina. These afflictions are beyond the owner's responsibilities, and their treatment, if one exists, is entirely in the hands of the vet.

But nothing excuses the owner who doesn't bother to clean the encrusted corners of his dog's eyes, or who doesn't go to the vet when he sees a yellowish pus coming form the eyes, or, worse still, who puts in a few eye drops from some solution that worked wonders a few months ago and was not all used up.

There are such things as criminal economies.

1   the American film by Michael Wadleigh, 1981

Basset Hound puppy

Touch

How sensitive a creature is to touch depends on the individual. Some animals, such as Belgian shepherds, don't like any contact with the bars of the jumps that they face during agility trials. Others, like Labradors, make light of banging into everything, as if it's a jinx. But every generalisation is a bit foolish; I know Belgian shepherds particularly insensitive to pain and very delicate Labradors.

In general, a dog is more than willing to poke his nose into everything. The burrowing reflex has taught him this behaviour. As an adult, he often resorts to it. His nose, a little like a finger, explores his surroundings. Of course his sense of smell takes priority but this doesn't tell him how solid a surface is, or the temperature of an object.

Especially when it's a new place, a dog prefers to explore the unknown by rummaging about with the tips of his paws. This is even more the case with strange creatures. How many hedgehogs, adders and cockroaches have perished under the claws of our dear four-footed companions...

Taste

We know that nature caters for all tastes. Sometimes though, with our cherished dog, it seems that nature caters for all that's distasteful! He unearths old putrefying carcasses, feats on the contents of dustbins and treats himself to bones with a sell-by date some months earlier.

The dog that lives in an apartment and can't get up to these little games will sometimes devour the droppings he finds on the route of his daily walk. All of this to the great despair of his owner, who has, wrongly, forgotten about prehistory. For genetically, mentally and physically, the dog is a carrion eater, a sneak thief, a street scavenger.

I was not there personally but I believe I know what went on in the avenues of the caverns occupied by our ancestor Homo Erectus.

Man had difficulty finding food. He broke open the bones of his prey to suck out the marrow himself. Work out for yourself what was left for the wolf-dogs that chose to become the first companions of our great forbears. Yes! Human excrement! This recycling temperament has been hardwired into the memory chromosomes of the dog, for good.

Moreover, the dog remains a carnivore. Even if he'll eat cooked vegetables and grated carrots, he persists in his preference for meat. Particularly meat that's been buried for some time, that's rotting – that is to say that decaying just a bit, covered in maggots, is a sort of natural cooking method. This preparation allows the food to be more easily assimilated.

Pyrenean Mountain Dog

These same dogs bury their bones or dead poultry and then dig them up again three months later, to feast on the rotten remains as if these had been prepared by Joël Robuchon himself. Their taste buds seem perverted to you? And what if they are right? Once again… Now don't shudder; even nowadays, man continues to hang pheasants and some game which he considers a particularly delicacy.

A form of kind medicine, instinctotherapy, asserts that an organism knows how to determine what it needs. Sometimes, we feel an overwhelming desire for cherries, cream buns, or black pudding. According to instinctotherapy, it is in our interest to obey these impulses. Popular wisdom accepts this to be the case for pregnant women, so why not accept the inner voice of nature for ourselves and for our dogs?

CHAPTER 6

Basic education is essential

'The puppy is father to the dog'

STEFEN.C RAFE

Basic education is vital. Unfortunately, some breeders claim that their puppies don't need one 'because they are so good and well-balanced.' That's like parents saying their children don't need to go to school. Nothing is more stupid. Every puppy needs to learn the boundaries of his own range of initiative and to have good manners; to know how to walk to heel with and without a lead, to come instantly when called by his master and to remain close by the latter during free walks. These four exercises constitute what I call the 'critical mass.' From then on, you can ask more and more of your dog, for your greater interest and his greater pleasure.

At what age should you start?

As soon as possible. I still sometimes hear people say that it is foolish to try and train a puppy, that this is equivalent to asking an infant in playschool to sit his high school diploma. Those who make this statement have no idea what a dog high school diploma actually is.

It goes without saying that, with a learner dog, you don't try to teach him how to guard a bicycle, to search and rescue, to refuse food in the master's absence, to act as lifeguard or to jump a ravine!

But up to the age of 5 months, when his adult teeth start growing, the puppy is in kindergarten. At this tender age, we can easily and accurately put the basic conventions into place. No puppy is already a domestic dragon and the master has not yet had time to make too many mistakes. You should know that a young dog is less malleable than a puppy. Often, he knows how to defend himself. At 18 months, he possesses the full physical force of an adult. He is fully developed mentally at 3 years old. At 7, he starts declining.

Up until what age can you start a good apprenticeship with a dog? Until the day he dies!

It is never too late. Often, in his old age, thanks notably to his long experience of living alongside humans, a dog becomes more flexible in spirit. That is just the time to make a spectacular improvement in him.

Life before Life

A puppy is created on the day mating takes place. Only the breeder can take any action at that moment. If she presents a bitch in good health, well rested, in perfect condition, that is to say vaccinated, recently wormed and on the skinny side rather than fat, to a well-balanced stud with a good family background, she makes sure the odds are stacked in her favour.

If, furthermore, the mother has a top quality temperament, is afraid of nothing and is not vicious, many of the conditions for making good puppies have already been met. The environment is the decider for the little being already in the warmth of its mother's womb. Just like for humans, if we talk to the embryo, the puppy will be more outgoing, more intelligent. Through the medium of liquids passing from the mother to the foetus, by the intermediary of the vibrations that traverse everything, the little being receives multiple influences. The breeder who talks to her pregnant bitch, who takes her out often, who lets her carry on working, within reason, during gestation, is fulfilling her duty well.

Good hunters don't deprive themselves of a good bitch as long as she can trot along beside them without getting too tired; the shepherds, in the mountains, don't leave pregnant females to carry on sleeping, on the pretext that they could wear themselves out. And these bitches produce offspring that is remarkably easy to train. Quite naturally, the puppies they create want to hunt or to guard.

If you can, go and see the bitch before you decide whether you want to take one of her puppies. It is she, not the stud, who will imprint the puppies with her behaviour, because she lives with them full-time. When the father also possesses many good qualities, notably good health and a solid character, the little ones will be good, almost certainly.

Remember, 'Dogs don't make cats.' To give birth to good puppies, it takes a good stud and a good bitch. There again, the buyer should check it out. And it's sometimes difficult.

If the breeder doesn't let anyone near her animals because she fears the ravages of an epidemic, or has mated her bitch to a champion in some distant country, or has called on the technique of artificial insemination to obtain the services of a stud that has been dead for several years, it becomes impossible to judge for yourself the qualities of the father. All that's left is to put your faith in the breeder, as usual.

Irish Wolfhound

Certainly, it happens that some declarations of parenthood are falsified and that some accidental matings happen without the breeder knowing, and the canine societies have no means of controlling everything, far from it. But, in general, breeders are honest. Furthermore, they are only too happy to offer a thousand detailed explanations of their breeding principles to anyone who asks.

By the intermediary of canine magazines and journals published by the breed clubs, you can amass piles of information on the breed you've chosen, and often on the actual parents of your future puppy.

In general, the breeder keeps the bitch close at hand or in her kennel. Some breeders, wanting to avoid having too many animals in the same place (given that epidemics and epizootic diseases can rampage through densely populated breeding kennels), entrust their bitches to competent friends for the period of gestation and suckling. This is also the case if they don't consider themselves to have enough time to look after each little individual properly. This way of going about things is perfectly respectable.

The maturation of the puppy

Experts believe that the first flush of a puppy's young life subdivides into three stages:-

1. The first two weeks constitute the neo-natal phase, which lasts until the puppy's eyes open. The animal seems deaf and blind. It hardly moves. In fact, its brain is not yet surrounded by the cortex, that shell containing the zones responsible for sight, hearing, touch, smell and co-ordination of movements. The spinal chord, through which the nerves pass on information, has little maturity. Only reflexes pass along it.

   The young animal sleeps 20 hours out of 24. He keeps in the warm, snuggling against his mother and his siblings. He is already familiar with paradoxical sleep; underneath his eyelids, the eyes blink rapidly, according to the rhythm known as REM (Rapid Eye Movement). He quivers, jumps, gives out meaningless noises.

   When he wakes up, he crawls towards a teat, which he kneads with his front paws. Towards the tenth day, he knows how to push on his front limbs and on the fifteenth, he starts to use his hind quarters.

   When his mother licks him underneath the tail, he urinates and defecates.

If you take a puppy out of the group, and put him on the ground, you will see that he has no sense of orientation at all. He wriggles about, rests his head on one side, turns around and utters piercing cries. He only calms down when he is back with his mother or with his siblings.

2. The third week represents the transition period, when the puppy's eyes open. This is when the jump reflex appears, provoked by noise, and this continues until the ears open.

The puppy still sleeps a lot of the time, between 15 and 16 hours a day. Half of this rest is taken up by paradoxical sleep.

The young animal moves about on its feet now, even if its hind quarters are not steady yet. He growls, barks sometimes. He starts to explore the kennel.

Towards the end of the third week, the upper canines appear. These little teeth in her young make the mother suffer. Pain makes her vomit. The little ones dive for this warm regurgitated paste, which gets them used to their future diet. The breeder starts them off on some very sloppy food, which the puppies swallow like adults, lapping it up.

3. From the fourth week until three months is the period for socialisation. Towards 1 month, sleep takes up no more than 8 or 9 hours a day, of which only 15% is paradoxical.

At 1 month, the puppy sees and hears normally. He wags his tail. Towards 6 weeks, the puppy can run. If he falls over, he gets up again quickly. He voids himself independently, without needing his mother to lick his tummy or the base of his tail. A puppy assumes the position of an adult female, crouching, back curved, hind feet tucked underneath the body, tail horizontal. At this age, he also sniffs out areas where others have done their business.

Environment plays a part, not huge perhaps but definitely a factor, from the day the mother is impregnated. It is however at the moment when the puppy starts to wag his tail, towards four weeks, that the world around him – objects, places, people, other animals – strikes his awareness with full force.

By wagging his tail, the young animal indicates his satisfaction in a manner visible to all. He plays more and more with his siblings; he sniffs them, bats them with his paw, chases them with better co-ordination each day. He explores the world, approaches whatever intrigues him, smells it, feels it with his teeth.

Our good breeder profits from this enthusiasm by giving him the maximum number of experiences. Until now the puppy has been in maternal care; now he goes on to playschool.

At five weeks, the first fights start up. The puppies bite each other's muzzles, necks, ears and start to defend themselves. The attacker is forced to let go. In this way he learns bite inhibition.

The puppy also begins to engage in defending an object; he puts his paw on the object of his choice, chews it, then growls and pretends to bite when anyone tries to approach him.

He discovers the 'Come and play' position, the one that is most likely to make his siblings want a game; belly and elbows on the ground, rump in the air, tail wagging, he gives voice while edging forwards or backwards.

At this age, no one puppy is dominant. During games, each one is alternately the winner or the loser. If there were one little scape-goat for his brothers and sisters, they would prevent him eating and he would die. The positions of dominance and submission are merely experimental; the vanquished lies on his back and the conqueror stands over him, pinning him down with front paws and continuing to chew at him.

Sometimes the little ones adopt the model of pack organisation, moving together towards the same target. They lick each other, mimicking the gestures of mating. Sometimes, in contrast, one of them will go off alone, to examine a toy by sniffing it, chewing it, or even shaking it to death.

Reflex actions

The normal puppy acquires a certain number of reflex actions at precise stages, in a fixed order. Basic behaviour does not vary. If you notice an anomaly, it is always the key to some problem of mental or physical health.

All normal puppies pass through each of the following stages;

1. Passive muscle tone. Take the animal carefully, with two hands, by the back of its neck and lift it up. From 0 to 5 days is the flexion phase, when the flexor muscles are the strongest and the little creature wants to roll into a ball. From 5 to 18 days, is the extensor phase when the extensor muscles take over, the puppy stretches his legs and arches his back. After 18 days, the animal achieves normotony, extensor and flexor muscles are in harmony, the legs move freely, the vertebral column has straightened out.

2. The hollowing reflex. If you enclose his muzzle in your hand, the puppy will move forward. It is enough to keep your fingers round his muzzle and pull your hand back a little for him to move forward several metres in this way, in pursuit of this funnel that steals away. The hollowing impulse permits the animal to remain in contact with the mother and her nursing. It disappears after the third week, to the advantage of more complex responses enabled by sight and the other senses.

3. The labial reflex. If you put your finger against the puppy's lips, he'll move his mouth towards the finger. This reflex disappears after three weeks.

4. The reflex for stretching and lengthening in opposition. Put the animal on his back, and gently pinch one toe of a back paw. The member touched will recoil and the other stretch out, to avoid the source of irritation. This reflex disappears towards the middle of the third week.

5. The Magnus reflex. The puppy stays on his back. Turn his head to one side. The members on that side stretch out; those on the other side recoil. This is true from birth until the end of the second week. During the third week, only the back paws react. After that, the Magnus reflex disappears.

6. The positional reflex. Position the puppy in front of the edge of a table and make him touch this with the sole of his

paw. Immediately, the animal lifts his paw and puts it on the table with the aim of moving forward and getting past the obstacle. This reflex appears towards the third day for front paws and at the beginning of the second week for the back ones.

7. The upright reflex. Lift the animal underneath his tummy, then, very gently, leave him standing. Between the sixth and the tenth day, the front legs stay straight. They are trying to support the body's weight. Between the eleventh and the fifteenth day, it's the turn of the back paws.

8. The voiding reflex. When the mother licks underneath the young animal's tail, he urinates and defecates. The response is the same if you touch the lower stomach of the puppy with your finger. As a matter of interest, this is the action used by an experienced breeder with orphaned puppies. After the fourth week, the voiding reflex disappears to be replaced by more controlled actions.

9. The standing reflex. If you lay the animal on his back, from the very first day he will try to turn onto his tummy.

10. The negative geotactic reflex. Place the puppy on a slight slope, head lower than body. From the first day, as long as the slope isn't slippery, he will try to turn around so that his head is higher up.

11. The thermal reflex. If the puppy is put in a cold place he will go completely bonkers. He calms down only when he is back in contact with a warm body, such as that of his mother or a sibling.

12. The gustative reflex. If you put a sweet substance on the puppy's tongue, he licks, sucks and swallows. With a bitter substance, he will grimace and produce lots of saliva in hopes of spitting out this disagreeable product.

13. The reflex where the eyelids contract on touch. Put your finger on the inside corner of the puppy's eye. In reaction, the animal closes his eyelids more tightly, right from the moment he is born.

14. The reflex for contracting his eyelids against the light. On the fourth day or later, the puppy should be able to squeeze his eyes tight shut if you bring a bright light close to them.

15. The photo-motor reflex. Towards 18 days, if you direct a beam of light towards the puppy's eyes when they are open, you can see the first movements of the pupils. These movements are still clumsy but they exist. Between the twenty-first and the twenty-fifth day, the young animal learns to turn his head towards a source of light appearing in the darkness.

Anatolian Shepherd Dog

16. The visual cliff-edge. This test should work on the twenty-eighth day at the latest. If you put the puppy on a table-top, near the edge, he should back away for fear of falling.
17. The startled reflex. Between 18 and 21 days for the first time, if you make a loud noise close to the puppy, he completely curls up into himself in self-defence.
18. The audi-motor reflex. Towards the twenty-fifth day, the puppy turns his head in the direction of the noise he hears.

A technological tool; the EEG

An EEG, or electroencephalogram, is presented in the form of a page, split into four parts, with a zig-zag line running across it. This shows the electrical activity of the cortex, the shell around the brain.

During his first week of life, regardless of whether the puppy is awake or asleep, the line remains virtually horizontal.

During the second week, periods of tranquil sleep are associated with a slight modification in the line.

The third week sees the appearance of a third pattern, which corresponds to periods of activity when awake.

The EEG testifies that, towards the end of the first week, the brain is aware of light being present and, eight days later, of a noise being made.

At the end of the seventh week, as we have already seen, the electroencephalogram of the young animal cannot be distinguished from that of an adult.

We can distinguish between about seventy reflexes and breeders are always trying to find out new ones. I have limited myself to the simplest, to those which anyone can see in action without using complicated resources. It is enough to take some common-sense precautions; handle the little ones gently, in a warm place, for no more than five minutes with any one puppy, avoid waking them up for the activities and be aware that the reflex actions only happen after a delay of a few seconds when the puppies are extremely young.

In the final analysis, there should be some leeway in the results for different breeds; the labrador for instance, which is a bit slower, more ponderous, than the Belgian shepherd, will take a few more days before showing a reaction.

Attraction and repulsion

These two opposite behaviours appear during the socialisation period. In practice, Nature, that prescient mother, has organised the maturation process as follows:-

1. From the second week onwards, the puppy is curious about his environment. He investigates his mother, his siblings, man. He is attracted by the surroundings in which he lives. This attraction occurs between the puppy and every species that he encounters. Experts talk of 'intra-species attraction' when the puppy is interested in other dogs, such as his siblings, and 'extra-species attraction' in other cases, with man, for example.

The very young animal retains only the characteristics of the various species, regardless of whether they are friends or foes. The individuals that he meets make no impact as particular personalities but rather represent their species with their behaviour. This is why the puppy forgets his breeder very quickly; he is only interested in this person as an example of the human race.

2. At the start of the fifth week a remarkable phenomenon occurs; the exhibition of attraction towards other species diminishes little by little, to disappear completely by the end of the third month. At the same time the dog learns fear and repulsion towards whatever is new. Having made sure that the young animal is not afraid of his own kind, Mother Nature wants to prevent him playing cute with his future prey or with his future predators and enemies.

This way the canine race will survive.

Deprivation and separation syndromes

The conscientious breeder must know how to make the most of these different stages in the mental life of a puppy; the variety of experiences offered to the young animal will determine the wealth of his intelligence, by their quality and quantity. Everyone can invent a thousand different games, walks, novelties, that will firm up the temperament of the young animal. All will be well, as long as there is nothing to fear and the animal is secure.

On the contrary, if the breeder thinks it enough to bring food once a day to the nursing female, without spending any time with her nor with the little ones, if no-one comes to see the litter, if the puppies never pay a visit to the vast world that is around them, if an orphaned puppy has no relations with other dogs, in short, if the young animal is deprived of contact, he will suffer from the shocking syndrome of deprivation which, in dogs just as in humans, can lead to nervous depression and death.

The dog affected by this syndrome isn't interested in anything, doesn't play, doesn't wag his tail, submits to any attacks, or bites anyone who approaches him, from fear. Tail between his paws, he huddles up in corners, walks in a tense manner when in unfamiliar surroundings. He doesn't go near anything new; another dog, a mirror, a man, everything scares him. He prefers simple objects; a box, a spot underneath the table. He licks himself till he draws blood. When someone hurts him, he is petrified. He finds the tiniest change in his environment intolerable. Experts have established that his threshold of homeostasis, his level of tolerance for noise, light or emotional assaults, is extremely low. He crosses this very quickly and suffers.

He is a world-class worrier. He has no social skills. He never goes exploring. Sometimes he refuses to eat for days at a time and lets himself fall into periods of total lethargy, of deep depression.

The blame for this problem falls almost entirely on the breeder.

Separation syndrome is almost as dramatic; the puppy can't get over his separation from the cocoon of his family. He doesn't understand why he's been taken away from the affection of his mother and siblings. If you encounter one of these miserable animals, tell yourself that he has been produced by a bad breeder.

Above everything, avoid a scared puppy!

When you choose your puppy, make sure he shows no fear when faced with a human being. In particular the young animal should not be scared of coming close to your shoes! In practice, bad breeders don't put up with little puppies nibbling the bottoms of their trousers and they are quick to nudge them away with their feet, even going so far as to kick them! Following on from this, these little puppies have already learned to fear man. They will present their future owners with all kinds of serious problems. Buyer, be very demanding at the moment you choose your puppy!

Desocialisation

But the owner can be responsible too. For, if it is possible to socialise a dog, it is also possible to desocialise it. It is enough to leave him to his own devices, shut up in a bleak environment, such as a kennel at the back of a deserted courtyard. Even if he is bought at 8 weeks after a good start in life with a competent breeder, this animal will pine. Even if he was appropriately socialised, good relations with other living creatures can deteriorate. Everything here depends on the determination of the owner. Do you want a top quality dog, well-balanced mentally and physically, resistant to diseases, and which is helpful in a thousand ways? If so, you have to offer him the chance to live in rich and varied surroundings. You have to put puzzles within easy reach and help him to find solutions. You have to keep on supporting him, letting him know clearly when you are pleased and when you are cross, so that he knows where he is, and you need to give him endless love and a wealth of cultural experiences. Love is the key word, the word that makes you want to devote time to your pupil.

Podhale Shepherd Dog

But love and time alone are not enough. You need to add a touch of technical know-how.

The rules of learning

Man finds it difficult to accept that other animal species, and therefore dogs, react differently from him when confronted with the same situation. For man and dog belong to two different worlds where they learn and survive by means of very different reactions.

Unfortunately, a dog often gives the impression that he is meditating in a human way. His expression so often takes on a human sparkle. And, like us, this little devil loves foie gras and fillet of beef, even if he needs a longer training to fully appreciate champagne or Waldorf salad.

The whole difficulty resides there, in this ambiguity and in the facility with which the master can distinguish subjective impressions from the reality. This is no easy task. You have to learn to understand dogs in general, and then yours in particular. As all the great trainers will confirm, even if certain traits are held in common, each dog has its own individual personality.

This complexity quite understandably prevents most trainers from writing books about training; they know that you never resolve the same problem in exactly the same way with two different dogs. The one exercise of walking to heel could take up an entire book, and we still wouldn't have exhausted all the possible approaches.

Nevertheless, as long as you're always in tune with your dog, and take heed of good advice, so as to put into action at any moment the technical know-how that seems to be most appropriate, there is much that you can teach, indeed an amazing amount that you can teach to your four-legged friend.

Learning has taken place, and further training, before the animal shows a sustained change in his behaviour, following repeated exercises or experiences.

Behaviour modification is internalised, controlled by the brain. But it can equally inculcate effects that are positive as negative, or indeed offer nothing at all to enhance the dog's life. It has to be sustainable. Changes in behaviour caused by fatigue or by flagging motivation indicate nothing about the training. Sustained modification comes either from training or experiences. If change comes from malnutrition, a growth spurt, or instinctive reactions, this cannot be called training.

The apprenticeship of the dog takes place according to certain natural laws, long understood. Some of these have a permanent effect, powerful, durable, capable of changing even blood pressure or sexual behaviour. For example, the Belgian Shepherd Dog, Robin de la Fontaine du Buis, had been so well trained to bite into protective clothing that he disengaged from a female on heat if a man playing attacker approached him. Robin preferred to chew padding rather than ensure the survival of his species!

The master should therefore know these natural laws, so as not to unwittingly set in motion harmful processes which could lead to the acquisition of unwanted habits.

Let's take, for instance, the case of the new owner who goes into transports of love for his dog every time he leaves the house. The master goes, the animal waits, then as the hours roll by, he eventually clamours for the return of his beloved master. To the extent that he barks all day long. A confident master leaves the house without saying a word to his dog. He doesn't make it a big event when he goes out. In this way, he avoids creating any tension.

In the same manner, his return in the evening is not an occasion for huge, noisy rejoicing. In any event, not in the first few minutes he enters the house. Someone who jumps around with joy when he gets home and greets his dog is sparking off a powerful negative consequence; an animal that barks, jumps and urinates with emotion on his master's return.

Better to start off well

I would a thousand times rather train a young puppy of 2 months to have good manners from the start than battle to correct bad behaviour, deeply embedded, in an adult. As the years have gone by, I have acquired a reputation for knowing how to put dangerous adult dogs back on the right track. So often, these animals have been the victim of learning all the wrong things.

Pavlov, Skinner and neuro-linguistic programming

Three modes of learning
1. Behavioural response of the 'bell-saliva' type. Pavlov's famous reflex, put to the test by this Russian expert, who systematically rang a bell before giving the dog his food. One fine day, the scientist noticed that the dog started to drool when he heard the bell, even if he received nothing to eat. This behavioural response disappeared quite quickly; the dog stopped salivating on hearing the bell if his master had stopped the routine of bell-food for a few days.

Mockers will however tell you the famous interpretation of events by Pavlov's dog, after several weeks of training; 'Why on earth does my master ring a bell as soon as I start drooling?'

Behavioural response is governed by a reflex of the nervous system. We speak of a 'conditioned reflex'. In general, the animal cannot control this reaction, which obeys the three phases of classical conditioning:-

- an event of no significance, known as a 'neutral stimulus'
- regularly presented to the animal just before an event of great importance to the dog, called the 'conditioning stimulus'
- then becomes, in itself, the cause of the reaction.

The dog hears the bell (neutral stimulus) and, almost at the same moment, receives his meal (conditioning stimulus). He will salivate also, but less, on other occasions, when he hears the sound of a different bell. This phenomenon is known as the 'generalisation from the stimulus.'

Dog-trainers frequently use this principle. The gun-dog, trained to retrieve a little wooden dumb-bell right to his master's feet, will in the same way fetch a freshly killed rabbit and bring it to him.

For classical conditioning to function well, the conditioning stimulus has to follow the neutral stimulus immediately. If Pavlov had brought the dog's dinner an hour after he rang the bell, the dog would have needed more than a few sessions to acquire the reflex of drooling at a tinkling bell! This is also true, quite clearly, in everything to do with training dogs. If you wait ten minutes before caressing your dog, after an impeccable recall to order, you can expect him to make his own mind up whether he comes back to heel or not.

Furthermore, if the neutral stimulus (the bell) is activated after the conditioning response (the food), the link between the two will never dawn on the dog and no learning will take place.

2. Operant conditioning, of the type 'lever-food', brought to light by the American psychologist, Thorndike. One day, he put a cat in a box that had a grilled opening, and a plate of food outside the box.

To open the door, the cat had to press down a lever situated near the door, inside the cage. Just by chance, from pacing up and down, the cat eventually pressed on the lever, and opened up its route to freedom.

Little by little, it learned to go straight to the lever and press it down as soon as it was imprisoned. Thorndike derived from this experiment his theory of 'the law of effect'; 'Behaviour is created according to the effects that it produces'.

Following on from this, Thorndike's American colleague, Skinner, defined the 'operant paradigm' in this way;

Learning is subdivided into three base components:-

a) a situation
b) a response
c) a sanction (punishment or reward)

Golden Retriever puppy

If, for example, the master repeats the word, 'Sit' without doing anything else and then if, by chance, the dog sits at that very moment, and then, in addition, the master rewards the animal with a tasty piece of liver pâté, it is probable that the next day, or the day after that, or after a month of this treatment, the dog will sit as soon as he hears the word, 'Sit.', and he will expect to receive his piece of liver pâté. If this doesn't work, then either the dog is stupid or he's not interested in the sort of reward on offer.

3. Neuro-linguistic programming. The two preceding theories have nowadays been incorporated in neuro-linguistic programming. The creators of this recent technique, intended for human use, started from a completely different point of view. They selected a number of individuals who had been very successful in their personal or professional lives, then they researched the characteristics that these people had in common. Their hypothesis? That it was enough to reproduce these behavioural characteristics to have the same success professionally and in relationships. An idea so simplistic seems to support the notion that Americans, inventors of this technique, are very naive. All the same, neuro-linguistic programming has proven itself to be very effective and the specialists who practise it are obtaining more and more precise results.

It is a more difficult technique to use in the reality of dog-training but some of my colleagues are trying their best to take it into account.

The two kinds of reinforcement

Reward and punishment together form what the experts call 'positive reinforcement'.

'Negative reinforcement' comes from disagreeable things and situations and provokes flight or avoidance. A typical example is that of the puppy who sees a burning candle, puts his muzzle on it, burns himself and learns this way not to get too close to a flame.

Primary and secondary sanctions

The term 'sanction' synonymous with 'consequence' covers both reward and punishment.

The primary sanction corresponds to the satisfaction of vital needs. An exhibitor who, for example, doesn't let her dog have anything to drink for the twenty-four hours before a show, and then, to make him look lively and awake, waves a little container full of water in the air about ten metres in front of the animal's muzzle while he is being presented to the judge, is calling on a primary sanction, relating to the satisfaction of a vital need, thirst.

The secondary sanction calls upon the mental possibilities of the dog, his higher emotions, such as his pleasure in being with his master. In the first place, a secondary sanction has no impact on the animal. It becomes effective little by little, after being associated with a primary sanction.

For example, what I call a 'verbal caress', that is a compliment along the lines of 'Well done, my little fleabag,' or 'That's great, you tub of grub, or 'Hello, pupsqueak!' I love these sweet nothings, with which you can be as creative as you like. But the verbal caress has no effect the first time it's used. It has to be repeated and associated with a friendly atmosphere before it takes on meaning. If you give your verbal caress at the same time as a piece of fruit or some liver pâté, or while you stroke him (a physical caress is a secondary sanction already familiar to the dog), then it will rapidly become fully effective.

American Staffordshire terrier

Some people hold that the difference between primary and secondary sanctions is difficult to establish with certainty. They assert, in particular, that affection is a vital need, as much so as hunger or thirst, and so affection cannot be considered a secondary sanction.

Be this as it may, but you will soon realise the virtue of the secondary sanction; it is a lot more easier to put into practice than the primary sanction, given that you don't always just happen to have some liver pâté with you.

The rhythm of sanctions

Rhythm has great importance in the use of a sanction. It has been demonstrated, a long time ago now, that a dog learns a new exercise very easily if he receives a sanction each time. This is known as the process of the 'continuous sanction'. But Skinner established with certainty another fundamental point; learning has its most durable effects if the sanction does not always automatically arrive, but rather if it is called on intermittently instead. This the theory of the 'intermittent sanction', the efficacity of which depends on two variables, the rhythm and the interval.

The experts speak of a 'fixed rhythm' if the sanction is given each time the animal has completed a certain number of exercises. So we speak of a rhythm 'fixed at 20' or 'FR 20', if the master caresses his dog once in every twenty times when the animal succeeds, for example, in bringing back a dead rabbit.

There is also the 'variable rhythm'. VR20 indicates that there is an average of one sanction, that is to say a reward or a punishment, for every twenty exercises.

If a dog scratches at the door with great conviction, he has probably been trained by the FR or VR method; his master, war-weary, has surely opened the door after suffering a number of scratching sessions. This form of training, by intermittent sanction, gives amazingly permanent results.

The interval between sanctions

The other variable is the time that passes between the action and the sanction. We speak of the 'fixed interval', or FI, or 'variable interval, or 'VI'. The dog who waits for someone at the dinner table to throw him a morsel of food is probably motivated by a 'VI'. He receives his treat, when allowed, after variable intervals.

Techniques based on variable intervals have proved more effective when linked with variation in rhythm. Unfortunately, behavioural problems are most often based on exactly this

variation in interval. They are therefore all the more solidly established and difficult to treat.

On the other hand, this works inversely too; the specialist who
puts a good habit in place can play on the interval between the
dog's good reaction and the reward given. I think that the only
secret of a good dog-trainer is the speed with which he gives the
appropriate response to a dog's action. The difference between a
good dog-trainer and an excellent one? A good one gives an
appropriate response in a tenth of a second, an excellent one in a
thousandth of a second.

Clearly both are working successfully; they give rewards
when the dog does well and reprimands when required. But the
better of two dog-trainers is the one who is the faster to opt for
the best solution.

Sanctions are more effective when they unleash a strong emotion; the morsel of liver makes a strong impact on a carnivore
which hasn't eaten for eight days but has little effect on one
which is getting twelve kilos a day! The sanction should be activated just after the act which motivates it. Precise experiments in
a laboratory have proved that the sanction is at its most effective
if it comes within a maximum of a demi-second after the act. To
delay a sanction is to encourage other behaviour, without meaning to do so.

Let's take, for example, the case of a young puppy arriving at
his new masters', in a badly soundproofed apartment, where it's
really not desirable that he is noisy. One day he happens to bark.
His master rolls his eyes at him, makes a pacifying gesture with
his hand and tells him in a soft voice not to bark any more. For
the young animal things are not at all clear; has he done well or
been naughty? He barks again. The master then decides to tell
him off in a louder tone and, finally, to shake him by the scruff of
the neck. But he carries out this punishment five or six seconds
after the dog has started barking, and so too late. This means that
the young animal, deep in his heart, believes the following;
'When I start barking, my lord and master doesn't tell me off. So
why the devil does he get wound up when I'm quiet? He probably wants me to carry on with the noise! I'm going to make him
really happy by barking my head off...' This is how you can

succeed, in the easiest way in the world, with a splendid example of inverse training, without you even realising.

It is enough to make the same mistake three or four times to embed it fully. To such a degree that it is preferable to give no sanctions rather than sanction too late.

Saturation

I have already spoken of the animal which is immune to both recompense and punishment because it has received them to saturation point. This phenomenon of saturation is evident with feeding certainly but also with caresses, encouragement and signs of disapproval.

Popular wisdom dictates 'Every weapon wears out.' If you want to avoid swamping your dog, it is best to keep to the following three principles:-

- Don't use treats as rewards if the training session takes place following a meal. In any case, it's better not to train a dog immediately after he has eaten.
- Change the reward frequently.
- Use small quantities of treats. Big enough to give the animal pleasure but small enough not to fill his stomach with the first reward.

  If the master is worried that treats will get his dog into bad habits, he need not worry. As long as verbal encouragements are linked with treats, these latter can very quickly be replaced by what I have called verbal caresses, which rapidly become equally effective.

Besides, learning is a process of accumulation. How firmly embedded an element of training is depends on how many times it has been repeated.

The principles of dog school

The best formula, that which I call induced training, consists of observing the animal, waiting until he does something we want him to, and then baptising that act at the moment the dog takes the decision to carry it out. For example, the dog starts to lie down and it's enough to say clearly 'Down!' After many repetitions, the dog lies down when given the order 'Down.' But you can't always leave it until the dog does something you want him to of his own accord. Especially when it's an adult dog that you need to redirect into good habits as soon as possible. You have to know how to arrange fate. For this reason, dog-trainers call on the technique of scaffolding.

Scaffolding

This is a matter of encouraging behaviours that are heading in the right direction, even if, at first, the dog is not working with any great precision. Little by little, the animal receives no reward unless he progresses further.

For example, to teach a young puppy the game of jumping through a hoop, the master first goes through a huge tractor wheel with his dog and congratulates his pupil warmly for this. The next stage is to caress the animal if he goes through the obstacle on his own. Then the dog is praised only if he jumps through a car tyre, the diameter much smaller now. Finally, he jumps through the proper version of a hoop without any problem at all.

Force and release

Specialists also employ the method of 'force and release' when they want to put new behaviours in place. Let's imagine that you want to teach your dog to sit. You press firmly on his rear end until finds himself sitting and you congratulate him.

Little by little, the training of the animal requires less and less pressure. The pupil sits more and more willingly because he knows a caress will follow. One fine day, a simple touch of a finger, then a gesture, then just one word, will be enough to obtain a 'Sit'.

Generalisation

A dog's brain has a permanent tendency to put routines into place. He loves to play the generalisation card, the outcome of the sort of stimulus I have already mentioned. This process of generalisation saves him a lot of energy but be careful; it can be very useful but also produces unwanted clutter at the same time.

Let's take the example of a spaniel, which has learned to return to its master and sit by him, on command. You only have to wait to find him saying to himself one day, 'Let me see... the last twice my master has called me when I was three metres from him; this time, I'm at three metres now so I might as well go back to him straight away because that's what he wants, for me to always go back when I'm three metres away.' Generalisation can lead to the inspiration underlying the following behaviour, of which I have not yet spoken, the dog that jumps stages.

Anticipation

A dog anticipates quickly. He tries to predict the short term reactions likely in his environment, including, of course, his master's requirements. This can result in catastrophes.

Let's take up again the case of the spaniel that returns from three metres away. If, one day, his master no longer pays any attention to him, thinking that the desired result has definitely been achieved, and if he doesn't insist on his dog returning to heel with precision, the dog will start thinking, 'Now this is really weird. What a crazy human. He doesn't know what he wants; he never knows what he wants; I might as well do what I want instead!' This is how you can find yourself with the most fugitive dog in existence, without even seeing the danger coming. He has learned to obey a little, then to disobey. And, believe you me, disobedience is really easy to elicit!

On the other hand, the skill of anticipation shows the master the high level of his animal's intelligence.

The limits of learning

The best dog-trainer in the world can't do everything. Neither science nor experience suffice to teach a dog to read Pushkin in the original text or to drive a bus. Like the most beautiful girl in the world, an animal can give no more than it has. It's therefore pointless, harmful even, to present your four-legged companion with a task that is beyond him. The animal must be endowed in his very fibre, by nature, with the capacity to carry out what you are asking of him. Some breeds are therefore predisposed to come to their master's defence; everyone thinks here of the German Shepherd Dog. Others, like the Portuguese waterdog, find it easy to retrieve the fish let slip into the water by fishermen unloading their boats. You could of course get a waterdog to attack someone but for that job, better to choose a rottweiler!

Interference

A spontaneous reflex can stop the animal using its brain. This is illustrated by the dog which cannot see or understand anything because it is so overwhelmed with the panic caused by a lightning flash.

Basenji

Ill health

Medical reasons can also stop some forms of learning. It is pointless to try to teach a dog with hip dysplasia to jump fences, when he is in the process of developing a painful paralysis of the back quarters. It is equally pointless to work on changing the behaviour of a bitch that urinates everywhere in an apartment if the poor little creature is victim of a raging cystitis.

As always, the absolute rule is to apply common sense. If you don't know how to tap into your dog's abilities to the very last drops, then limit yourself to demanding regular everyday things, without excess.

Frustration

Arrange things in advance so that your pupil really wants to do whatever it is you have in mind. Motivate him, increase what the experts call the 'specific appetence' then frustrate the pleasure resulting from the exercise in store. Organise things so that the animal's instinct is deeply unsatisfied. And then let that instinct act. Everything will then work together for an action that is rapid, clean, precise.

For example, for a recall to heel, one of the best systems is to give the lead to a friend, then distance yourself while calling playfully, 'Lucky, here, here, here, little fluffball, here my Lucky!' When you have disappeared into a hiding-place, the friend drops the lead. Everything makes it likely that Lucky will arrive at a gallop, thanks to his hunger for his master.

Motivate but always in moderation. Frustration that is too strong can lead to psychologically disturbed behaviours. The dog can choose 'substitution'; if his master totally forbids him to bark, he can urinate on the feet of chairs instead!

He could also adopt the solution of 'displacements' and do something completely different from what was expected of him, such as scratching himself until he bleeds.

Some animals, faced with too great a frustration, develop all kinds of organic insanities in reaction to the mental over-stimulation that they are receiving. They physically destroy themselves.

Veterinary surgeons know very well the eczemas and arthritic or muscular rheumatism coming from stress that is too overpowering for the animal to bear.

Playing on a dog's motivation, is a bit like hitting a distant target with an elastic catapult. If you stretch the elastic correctly, the result is good. But if the elastic is too taut and breaks, you'll get a stone in your eye!

Spitz

The resultant of excitations

You should moreover be wary of that phenomenon, still little recognised, that can equally prove to be the best and the worst of things. The principle is simple; instead of substituting some exercises for others, different approaches can multiply their effects.

Let's take the case of training a dog to pull a cart, like a sled but with wheels. At first, you put the animal, wearing its harness, in front of the vehicle, which is in drive mode. The master walks ahead and calls the dog, who wants to rejoin his protector and so pulls the cart. End of Phase One.

Next, the master teaches his four-legged companion the technique of going ahead. The master gives the order 'Go ahead!' and when the dog dashes off straight ahead to find the ball that has been hidden a hundred metres away, he has the cart attached to him. He is therefore pulling it from then on with his master behind him. End of Phase Two.

After that, you include the animal in a practical session with a majority of experienced dogs. By imitation he now pulls the cart along just by copying the other dogs. End of Phase Three.

Different techniques provide mutual reinforcement through combining the appeal to different learning styles. A dog taken successively through each one of these methods will be better at pulling a cart than an animal dependent on just one technique of learning.

The theory of combining approaches based on different learning styles also asserts that, if the same signal is delivered by many sources at the same moment, or by one source in many different forms, it has a much stronger effect. So don't be afraid to approach the same exercise from the viewpoint of different methods. The desired action will be induced much more easily.

But beware the two enemies of this invaluable weapon; inconsistency and fatigue

Inconsistency

First enemy; inconsistency. If you change method every day, or as soon as you encounter a new theory, the dog won't understand anything. A good rule of thumb is to persevere for a month with the method you have chosen before changing to another.

Fatigue

Second enemy; fatigue. The stronger the stimulation, the more it demands from the dog's organism. This even more true when the animal is young. Mental fatigue, acting on the nerves, is less visible but just as strong, as, if not more than, physical tiredness. To carry on with the intention of working a dog that has exhausted its desire for action is a form of abuse and is likely to put him off working in future sessions.

Hitting

To hit a dog is to train it to bite you!

Let's take the example of slapping the animal across the head. The scenario behind the blow is sub-divided into three phases:-

1. The hand is coming. The dog pulls back his head, readying its neck to strike in the pose of a snake prepared to bite.
2. The hand touches the dog's head.
3. The hand withdraws. For the dog, this looks like prey fleeing. And, in the ancestral reflex, the dog is urged by nature to catch and bite any animal that flees!

Furthermore, I believe that Phase 2, when the hand makes contact, is like squeezing the trigger on a gun.

Don't hit your dog, not even with a newspaper rolled into a tube, with a strap, or with a bath towel. Don't even threaten to hit him. For the mechanism is always exactly the same; when you hit him, when you threaten to hit, you are unleashing the ancestral mechanisms of a carniverous predator. And don't listen to all these self-declared experts who assure you, 'A good beating and everything will be sorted.' The day when your dog becomes dangerous thanks to such stupid advice, the same 'experts' will encourage you to have your four-legged companion put down.

When people bring me a dangerous dog, I trace back the history of this animal's life, and I always find he has been hit. Not necessarily vicious blows, but physical punishment all the same.

Shouting

If one of your bosses hurled a continuous stream of abuse at you, would you feel great respect for him? Would you try to do better at what he asked of you? No, of course not! So don't shout at your dog when you give him a command. And don't shout, 'Shut up!' when he's barking too much. Unless you want to offer the spectacle of two creatures barking their heads off.

To be obeyed, it is really important to send positive messages. This is nothing to do with shouting but rather a matter of showing your four-footed companion that you are not joking. Rest assured that, even when you speak in a soft voice, your dog can hear you perfectly. Clearly there are limits to even the extraordinarily discriminating ear of your dog. Over a long distance you'll have to give full voice to be heard. However, if, at a normal speaking distance, you shout every time you give the tiniest command, you will have nothing left in reserve in case you really need to raise your voice.

Don't get your dog used to being shouted at. The only manner of doing this is to avoid shouting all the time. This needs you to learn to control yourself. This quality is as essential to a good master as is technique.

Dogs beyond redemption

I know what I'm talking about here. In 'Les Bichons', Catherine Baziret said I was considered to be 'a magician' in training dogs (which is not true; there is no magic, just a little technique and some good resources and my methodology works just as well with all the dogtrainers in my dogmasters.com team). So, veterinary surgeons or breeders send us 'dogs beyond redemption'. They can always be redeemed, in fact, but they have come within a whisker of the final solution.

I will say this again; every time, when we find out the background of such a 'dog beyond redemption', we discover that somebody, perhaps the master, on the advice of some 'expert' rubbish-monger, has hit this dog and shouted plenty of times.

Do not hit your dog, ever! Don't shout when he is there!

When you hit him, when you shout, you put yourself in the dog's playing field; in this game of 'hit the hardest', or 'shout the loudest', he is far more gifted than you are.

CHAPTER 7

The techniques of canine education

'Make sure it isn't the dog that successfully trains the master,'

ANDRÉ NOËL

The signals

Between dog and man, nature continuously weaves a dense network of signals that are more or less invisible, more or less difficult to decode, above all for the two-legged animal, who relies above all else on the one tool, speech.

The dog compensates for his lack of verbs by his fine analysis of the behaviour of the people around him and, in particular, of the most important being in his world, his leader of the pack, his master.

I like to call this capacity for analysis 'canine vocabulary'. The companion dog, which lives in the house all the time, and the champion working dog both possess an extensive canine vocabulary. The dog's 'passive' vocabulary, that is to say his understanding of the signals he receives is, like that of man, almost twice as rich as his 'active' vocabulary, that is to say the whole collection of signals that he himself gives to the outside world. It is man's responsibility to correctly interpret the messages given him by his four-footed companion.

Right the way through these pages dedicated to techniques, I will keep coming back to the signals linking man and dog. As soldiers are aware, the lines of communication are the commander's key weapon. The master has won when he manages to establish links between the dog and himself, to his advantage.

For education is really nothing more than the establishment and maintenance of this communication, of the code by which they live together.

To attain this objective, the essence is that a good signal is a signal sent by the master to at least one of the animal's five senses. A good signal needs no support from artificial instruments. The dog perceives it clearly; it interests him. Under certain conditions, the master can send the signal from a distance. There should be no possible confusion in interpretation.

The master should then accumulate a collection of good signals, well differentiated, adapted to the diverse reactions that he wants to elicit from his pupil and to the diverse situations of the real world.

Putting the five senses to work

A real master seeks to understand, and to make the most of, his dog's five senses. Every dog and every human has a unique personality. The quality of their partnership is largely determined by the more intelligent, that is to say, the human. I am not asserting here that the human is always more intelligent than the dog but I do believe that he carries the responsibility for any failure. It is therefore up to him to take the initiative.

For communication with his pupil he has at his disposal the familiar tools of hearing, sight, touch, smell and taste. Each one of these senses is capable of transmitting a specific signal, but not the definitive message, the one that will say everything. Each sense has weaknesses that limit its usefulness; no-one will attract his dog's attention in the pitch black of night, using only gestures.

Hearing

The master continually resorts to his dog's hearing. Use of the voice presents four major advantages:-

1. It is an everyday tool for a human.
2. It is always available.
3. You can make use of it instantly.
4. It works over a distance.

Of course, if the distance is too great, the voice becomes less effective, which is why trainers and shepherds have systems for the use of a whistle. And various inventors have thought up radio-transmission collars with loud speakers that carry his master's voice to a dog across hundreds of metres.

The uninitiated often imagine that the voice transmits words and that the dog understands these words. In reality, our four-footed companion only takes in the significance of the tone. It is the musicality that he understands.

I have already referred to the following experiment; if your dog obeys the order 'Down!' and you try saying ' Rain!' in the same tone, and using the same body language, he will obey you. He will have understood your music. And your gestures...

Remember, there is no point shouting. Keep to your normal speaking voice but infuse it with energy. A teacher knows that when she goes to class having lost her voice, all the pupils end up speaking in soft voices by the end of the day! On the day you really need to shout, to demand an instant drop into the 'down' position that will save your dog's life when he is about to run across the road towards you right in front of an oncoming car, then you will pat yourself on the back for your good habits. On that day, your dog will obey you instantly, because he will sense the urgency when you shout. If you shout all the time, he won't notice anything special about this particular command.

That having been said, you still need to choose your words. Clear ones are best, well-differentiated according to the exercises. At first, always say each one with the same intonation. It is your tone that will convey your meaning.

'Slowly!' pronounced in a drawl, 'Ssss-loooow-lyyyyy' will positively slow down a dog that's trying to overtake you, especially if you slow down at the same time you say the word.

'Search!' pronounced in an encouraging and tranquil tone, will re-motivate an animal tired of tracking.

'Well done, what a good dog!' in an enthusiastic tone expresses how pleased you are, with no ambiguity.

Words can be backed up by tone of voice. They can also be accompanied by gestures, which appeal to another of the dog's senses, that of sight.

Sight

From the moment that you can get your dog to look at you, think about your use of gestures. Don't forget that your four-footed companion spends his life trying to decode your mannerisms. Visual signals have five big advantages.

1. They prevent the master shouting.
2. A dog that is well-trained to pick up visual commands is very attentive because he can't rely on waiting to hear an order, something he can do while looking elsewhere. He has to remain focused on his master all the time.
3. Some actions transmit very clear messages and can therefore be used on their own. Think, for instance, of crouching in front of your dog and putting your palms on the ground, an action that is generally enough to command a 'Down'.
4. Like the voice, actions are always available to the master and can be put to work without any preparation.
5. Body language can carry over a long distance. We should remember that the dog sees movement very well, even that of a tiny animal. It is in his interest to do so; in the wild, the wolf feeds mainly on mice!

Gestures as commands

Choose the gestures for commands according to the following criteria:-

- the ease with which you remember them (the master has to easily recall the movement he has decided to use in each particular case).
- the clarity of differentiation (every gesture should be characteristic, to avoid the animal confusing it with another one).
- the possibility of being seen (be careful about distances; movements should be large if you're going to be far away) Think also about background colours, in which gestures can disappear if you're wearing clothes of the same shades.

Training by gesture suffers however from two major weaknesses:-

Bouvier de Flandres

- in the first place, the dog might very easily not see a gesture. All it takes is for the animal to be attracted by some distraction interfering at the very moment that you move. While his hearing is almost omni-directional in operation, his angle of vision is limited to a fan-shaped section, which, although larger than that of man's, is still quite limited. Besides which, in certain activities, such as cart or sled pulling, where the animal doesn't look at all at the master behind him, visual orders are obviously no use.
- above all, the master has to learn to control his gestures carefully, to suppress superfluous movements, if he wants to effectively take and keep the status of leader of the pack. A competent leader doesn't behave like a madman, he keeps his sang-froid in a storm or a domestic upset.

Experts in communication by gestures have named their specialty 'metacommunication' or 'non-verbal communication'. Unconsciously, every animal – and that includes us – reacts instinctively to the attitudes presented by those he encounters. This is the essential theoretical contribution of neuro-linguistic programming. Do we prepare for discussion when faced with someone whose arms are firmly crossed? Without meaning to, without knowing it, we adopt the classic reaction of defense or aggression when faced with this closed, rigid posture. Do we approach someone who is smiling, whose arms ands hands are open? We automatically respond in a friendly way, with warmth. In some jobs, such as public relations, the fashion industry, advertising, the principles of such 'infra communcation' are well understood as, in these circles, they know that the tiniest details count. Your smile, your relaxed attitude, your arms open to show a welcoming frame of mind, achieve more than force or temper in training a dog to bond with his master.

A smile? Of course! Smile at your dog. He is not stupid. He knows what this means. He understands you better than you would ever imagine. Show him tenderness in your behaviour. You will be repaid, more than amply. And very quickly.

Touch

You can also make use of touch. Some dogs are more sensitive to it than others. Belgian Shepherd Dogs, for example. They are upset if they brush an obstacle while jumping over it so they make an extra effort to jump higher at the next attempt. The master can profit from using his hands, especially to obtain obedience early on. With your hands, you can, with total control, pass on messages gently or with more firmness. Your hands can fine-tune their effect. But, even if they are always available in the field, they have the disadvantage of a very short range. They can hardly reach beyond a metre. It is therefore in your interest to use accessories which extend your hands' sphere of influence.

The tool most used on training grounds is the lead. 2. 20 metres right to the hand, without a grip, without a clip, ring or clasp. You can make this prop with almost anything, from polypropylene string to a good leather strap. As long as you make sure that the material and the clip attaching it to the collar are strong enough. What I do myself is to make a polypropylene strap. This will take a weight of 1200kg, well beyond any dog, even when full of high spirits. I attach this to a solid chain collar, again for reasons of its resistance. But I never attach it as a 'choke chain'. And I never use a spiked collar of the sort known as 'Torquatus'.

The lead, which becomes a long line when it is longer than three metres, is in my eyes the most indispensable tool when you have a dog. The famous dog-trainer, André Noël, tells anyone willing to listen, 'A professional trainer always keeps his dog on a lead'. You might not be a professional dog-trainer but it is always a good idea to have a lead with you.

Training or torture?

Nowadays, some people use electrical appliances in the practice of dog-training. Tele-Takt in Germany, Tritronics Pet Safe in the United States are collars which, thanks to a radio receiver and a generator, a 'torture machine', inflict a mild or more intense electric shock on a dog that is disobedient or that makes a mistake. Without having to move an inch, the controller can just push the button on his remote zapper. Clearly this resource sends an instant message, and with some power! It does though have two disadvantages:-

- Despite all the electronic protection systems, nothing will ever stop it being activated by accident, perhaps by a badly insulated moped or by a signal sent during military maoeuvres, wrecking in this way all the work that has been accomplished.
- Because it is apparently so effective, the master tends to over-use and abuse it. Instead of reflecting on the fine detail, he hits the zapper. I have seen people frenetically pushing a button while their dog, a few hundred metres away, somersaults like a kid-goat without understanding what his master wants from him.
- And American researchers have discovered that the electrical charges received by dogs provoke micro-bubbles all along the nervous circuits, on the spinal marrow and in the brain, in a similar way to what happens in a car battery.

What matters is to choose the least of all possible evils. What do you do when a dog barks like crazy all day long in an apartment, or at every single passer-by, and nothing calms him down apart from an electric collar? Is it better to have him put down?

Different options exist nowadays; a collar that squirts smelly or cold substances, or emits only unpleasant noises to a greater or lesser degree, or variations on all these effects. The choice is a personal matter.

Smell

This is it, the greatest area of disagreement and misunderstanding between man and dog. We have seen that, if the former is 'nose-blind', the latter has a scent organ capable of astounding performances. The American dog-trainer, Linda C. Franklin, states that her Tervueren can smell the difference between a one-dollar and a twenty-dollar bill. Perhaps she's exaggerating a little but it's a good story!

Not really having a sense of smell, man doesn't think to call on that of his four-legged pupil, except in certain exercises of advanced training, and, obviously, in tracking. People training blind dogs know how to make regular use of scented markers to enable these poor creatures to find their way around despite their disability.

Taste

The situation is not that much better regarding the use of taste. You can use treats to obtain certain responses. Unless this constitutes a serious training fault in the particular ringsport programmes in which the dog competes. A dog which is often going to be presented with the exercise of food refusal should not be rewarded with treats during training.

Experts know that a dog's sense of taste exhibits some bizarre characteristics. Do you want to teach him not to eat something lying on the ground so you resort to pepper, mustard, tincture of bitter aloes lining one or two pieces of booby-trapped bait? Very quickly, you'll realise that the dog will swallow everything all the same, and often ask for more…

How to pass on messages

We have seen which of the animal's receptors can be sought out by man for his messages. But how do you make sure that the message is clearly perceived?

In the conventional method, the trainer
1. gives a verbal message.
2. behaves in such a way as to get the desired response from his pupil.
3. sanctions the animal with a kind word, a caress or a treat if he gives the right response or a punishment if he makes a mistake.

In this method, Phase 2 can take two forms; constraint or enticement.

Let's take a simple example. The master says, 'Sit!' then obliges the dog to sit by pushing hard on his rump – the constraint method – or holds a piece of cheese above his muzzle to make him lift his head so that he automatically sits of his own accord to be more comfortable. This is the enticement method.

Trainers resort alternately to these two fundamental strategies; constraint or enticement. The results are good and rapid, but it is difficult to decide what dose of each ingredient to give. The more quickly and durably you succeed in this fine judgement, the better a master you become.

Nowadays, there is a third way; induced training or the 'association method'. This new concept, adapted from research carried out in the United States by some animal psychologists, has more and more followers, particularly in the somewhat closed circles of competitive obedience, the sport where a dog learning obedience is pushed to the level of a real form of art.

The master observes his dog attentively. He waits until the dog presents the desired behaviour, or starts to do so. At that exact moment, he gives the command to carry out exactly what the dog is just about to do. So, for example, when the dog watches his master preparing a beef casserole and starts to sit, the master orders, 'Sit!' and congratulates him heartily for having obeyed so well. From association of ideas, the dog, one fine day, sits when he hears, 'Sit!' even if, on that occasion, he hadn't been about to sit at all! This might seem surprising but this technique works very well, with a co-operative dog.

The only qualities that you need here are patience, attention and some experience of canine mannerisms, allowing you to recognise the clue that tells you what your dog is just about to do. You need to train yourself to read your dog's mannerisms and sequences of actions. In return, the association method maintains and develops the desire to obey the master. The dog perceives the command as an order he would give himself. There is no physical constraint to disturb or frighten him.

Obviously, it is preferable to start with a very young puppy and to limit the actions and orders to those which culminate in fun and pleasure like 'Go play with the ball!', 'Come here so I can cuddle you!' or which are unambiguous such as 'Sit!', 'Down!' and for short, complete actions.

At first, prioritise the naming of the objects and activities that the dog likes. If he grabs a ball, say 'Ball, ball, that's your ball, my sweetie-pie, your ball.' By this method, you get the young animal to associate certain words with certain objects, and with pleasure.

Specific messages can, with a dog really familiar with his master, lead to a thorough labelling of objects and actions. Experts have established that a dog has a vocabulary of three hundred words. In my view, that's a minimum.

When you introduce new words and commands, they will be received in a positive atmosphere. The dog will say, 'What the leader suggests is always great fun, so this will be too. When I understand what he's telling me, I will have even more entertainment.' Then he will do his best to try to decode what you are

Welsh corgi

telling him. In this way you will teach your dog to want to understand you, to love learning.

One inconvenience; the association method hits a natural limitation. It is no use for actions the dog doesn't like or doesn't do voluntarily. If you are waiting for an aggrieved dog to enter, of its own accord, the compartment where you want to wash him, you risk the bath-water evaporating completely before you've shampooed the animal! In this situation, better to go back to the good old traditional methods; constraint and enticement. For the day will inevitably come when, having aged a few months, the young animal will show you that, actually, he doesn't want to obey you any more. He will play deaf, he will show you his rear end, he might even display his fine teeth! Everything will indicate that it's time to return, temporarily, to constraints. Let him know that you haven't abdicated and that you still retain, always, the leadership of the pack.

Be careful as the induced method doesn't fit in with an hour's training here and there. It is rather a permanent philosophy to which you can resort when the opportunity presents itself, that is to say at any time. Thanks to this method, obedience and a sense of responsibility become a way of life not just artificial and fleeting behaviours.

This modern method is particularly attractive to people who make use of training in daily life not just in competitions.

Gradually, from the approach of different methods, that you might use alternately depending on your preferences and your mood, you will lead the dog into ever more complex actions, such as guarding the house or bringing the newspaper to the master, sitting in his chair.

Chain reaction

Thanks to the technique of the 'chain reaction', where you associate voice with gesture, you can lead your dog into various transfers of obedience. For example, a puppy has learned to come when you command, 'Come here!' One day, you add 'Heel, come here.' After several training sessions, you delay saying the 'Come here'. The animal rapidly understands. He runs to you before the 'Come'. Praise him. You have succeeded in the transfer. You can also move, in the same way, from verbal commands to gestures.

Chain reaction allows the teaching of complex orders, such as how to crawl. It is enough to demand, 'Down' and 'Come here' at the same time. One specific gesture, perhaps a zig-zag with an open hand, can accompany the verbal commands in order to stand on their own completely at a later stage.

Half-commands

Over time, it is in your interest to adopt this technique. In practice, at night, in your sitting-room, you probably won't require a perfect 'Down' from your dog. The command, 'Down' will lose its hallowed nature if you use it at every drop of a hat. So why not use specific terms, not linked with unequivocal obligation? For example, 'Over there!' could mean 'Find yourself a nice peaceful corner, stay there or shift about a bit, I won't tell you off as long as you don't get up!' In this way you will preserve true commands from being watered down as quickly as the frequency with which you use them.

As for me, when I want to see my dog beside me, I make a little 'Psssht' noise. I certainly don't want to demand that he permanently walks to heel in French National Championship mode. When I think it's time for him to head off again, I don't forget to tell him, 'Go on then, go and play!' I'm the one who decides when the exercise is over, not the dog.

Exercises for independence

The dog is a creature of habit. For him, certain tasks, in particular defending his master, take precedence over all the rest. Commands to a guard dog shouldn't always take on an imperative form because a real criminal isn't going to wait until you've put the dog into his defensive state. The animal has to know he can take decisions. Don't pick on him all the time on the false pretext that you are controlling him to perfection. In the ring, there is some benefit in using a few half-commands with flexible outcomes, that don't insist on rigid obedience. The course for protection dogs working in the countryside lasts three-quarters of an hour. There is no way you can have your dog impeccably to heel for all that time. Many masters therefore establish a private code with their work-mate. They say something like 'Come here old boy,' which means, 'This is a breathing space linking two workshops, so don't blow a gasket concentrating now and working yourself into the ground. Relax a little, chill out, but don't go too far away.' Every weapon gets used up, every command too. Over-use of orders is definitely the most common cause of lack of obedience.

Orders to work

Orders to work leave the animal plenty of scope for initiative and to take decisions. 'Search and bring it back!', when tracking, means 'Go and get on with it!'

In sheepdog trials, or hunting, or in the life of a guide-dog, people frequently use orders to work. They show the animal that you're serious, that it really is necessary to go to the coal-face, but that you don't have to be omnipresent in all the sequences of his actions. Orders to work even contain at times the implicit authorisation to disobey in case of need. If the sheepdog sees the sheep heading for a deep gully that the shepherd hasn't seen, he can and should stop, or drive the herd of sheep at an angle despite the order, received at the start of the day, to go straight ahead.

Shar Pei puppy

Working orders rest more lightly on the dog. Moreover, they suit his natural tendency to go about his business calmly. To prevent him changing commands to working orders, of his own accord, there is an effective solution; only the fomer lead to caresses, praise, treats. The latter elicit no particular notice from the master.

One last word; don't repeat a command. You give it once, not twice. In any case, if a command isn't working, it won't become effective by repeating it. How many times have I seen owners wear their lungs out with 'Down, come on, down, down, my good dog, down!' Apart from being ridiculous, this habit of repeating commands over and over has a really bad consequence; it teaches the dog to disobey. At best, the dog obeys after the fifty-third command.

If you repeat a command, you lose face. Your dog is learning to negotiate with you. To repeat a command is to teach your dog not to obey straight away! In addition to commands, you can also send various messages to your dog:-

- permission to charge into an action which you can see tempts him strongly, like jumping into the car boot for example.
- an invitation to change activity, pronounced with question intonation, 'Do you want to play?'

One disadvantage of the question; the master never knows what the dog really wants in his heart of hearts. The incontrovertible consequence is that if the dog doesn't respond as hoped, the master can't then hold him to the action. 'You want to go for a walk, Prince?' If the 'Prince' in question remains obstinately at your feet, he shouldn't receive any reprimand.

Congratulations

Send out encouraging signals the moment the animal starts to act in the way you want. Don't hesitate to encourage the animal even in the middle of an action. Let him know that his master is content, that all is going well and that he should carry on as he is.

You can be sure of one thing; the best rewards, for a dog, are kind words, the good vibrations coming from your very being.

Messages like these can't be bought. They have far more value for your pupil than all the treats in the world.

And – horror of horrors – I own up to thinking that caresses are harmful gestures. Yes. Because we don't give enough! They make us believe that we have done our duty because we have given Tootsie a good cuddle this morning. It is not enough; far more is needed.

Contrary to the action of a caress, a discreet, 'Well done, pup-squeak,' doesn't require you to stop what you're doing. And you can repeat it twenty times an hour. Long live congratulations, your best tools for dog-training!

Punishments

Messages of reprimand are the exact inverse of signals showing satisfaction. They are meant to show the pupil that he has made a bad choice either in one of his independent decisions or after an order. Everyone can choose his own signals to act as reprimands.

However, I strongly advise people to adopt gentle reprimands to start with, and draw back from them as quickly as possible after a gradual escalation in punishment. For many people, the word, 'Training' is confused with 'Breaking-in'. You need to keep control, certainly, and sometimes tighten it. But I repeat; use the minimum constraint necessary.

Physical Constraint

If it comes to this, it is governed by three absolute rules:-

- Always choose the kindest interventions. A simple, 'Tsk!' can usefully replace more severe actions. For the most part, dogs are not sad idiots. They understand things very well when you appeal to their intelligence. Furthermore, gentle constraint doesn't panic them and so doesn't block their capacity to learn.
- Don't stay at the same level if that has no effect. It is imperative that you up the ante in constraint, instead of

limiting yourself to repeating the same thing. This escalation should make an increasingly strong impression, strong enough to crack even the hardest. It is for this reason that you have to start at the lowest level and progress as slowly as possible.

- Give in as soon as the animal gives in. When you have found the level necessary to be effective, don't go any further. If the dog sits when you put your finger on his rump, why tap him to get a 'Sit'.

If you give yourself over to constant and ill-judged use of force, you lose the option of using it on an occasion when it is really necessary. The truth is that the dog has an extraordinary capacity to tolerate what we would consider to be extremely painful. I have seen champions from the ringsport receive a continuous stream of phenomenal thrashings ... and go back for more. Don't let yourself fall into this trap of resorting every time to physical pain as part of training. Be careful as many dogs unfortunately give the impression that they love getting hit. When you're an old hand at the training grounds and have seen it all, you start to wonder exactly what will truly hurt a dog.

My thinking does not come from squeamishness. It is based purely on reasons of effectiveness. By keeping constraints to the lightest possible level, you keep in reserve the possibility of acceleration. It is for each person to define his own signals of constraint. Here as in everything else, every neutral signal, the drone of a motor for example, might convey a reprimand. It only suffices to have charged this noise with negative meaning, by the principle of the chain reaction.

And don't be afraid of your pupil's mistakes. Don't be cross with him. Long live the mistake! It allows you to let your dog know when he's got something wrong. He will succeed tomorrow or another day. Keep a positive, patient attitude. With a well trained dog, you can even provoke a mistake artificially now and then, to reassure yourself that he will never again – or hardly ever – disobey you.

The dog that doubts

Never let your dog wait for your opinion. Far better to tell him a thousand times that he is gorgeous and he should just keep right on as he is, rather than wait for the end of the exercise before praising him. You will risk distracting him a little at first but that's not a serious problem.

You can resort to various signals to show him that you are pleased; a soft purr or a caress with the tip of the index finger on the rump can usefully replace words. I have already shown how you can achieve this desirable outcome thanks to the technique of the chain reaction.

As for reprimands, the same thing goes; don't wait!

The release command

In general beginners are good at giving the initial command, 'Down!' for example. But the majority of would-be trainers are surprised to see their pupils lie down, then get up and disappear out the door. The dog has not learned to obey right up to the moment the master decides that the exercise is over, saying something like, 'OK, go and play.'

If you give an order at the beginning then you must give an order at the end. If you don't respect this rule, you can't train a dog properly.

Active walks

I firmly believe that the beginner will gain time if he makes himself build patiently, moving calmly from the simple to the more complex. And in a good mood. For, contrary to what most people think, training can take place with a great deal of pleasure. An animal which has been mentally driven to exhaustion by a brutal, crude and stupid handler, is not going to work well. He is just a mechanical slave, incapable of taking the initiative. He frequently suffers from various afflictions; eczema, digestive problems, unhealthy coat etc.

One of the best opportunities to practice training in all

kindness, is on a walk. Allocate a good hour each day to walking calmly in a peaceful place where you can let your dog off the lead. Without appearing to do so, slip some short periods of work in from time to time, without the animal even noticing. It is better to do twenty little exercises of ten seconds walking to heel rather than twenty minutes with nothing but this exercise.

During the walk, you will find dozens of pretexts for a training exercise, in an informal way at first, then with more and more precision to the extent that you have made progress.

A chopped-down tree trunk or a heap of tiles are chance obstacles to create a little challenge for a gutsy dog. A meeting with a strange dog gives you the chance to test how effective the recall is. And if you hide while your young animal is investigating a butterfly, you will make him use his nose to find you again, and to concentrate more on you.

This active walking presents a secondary advantage; the master and the young animal get to know each other while completely relaxed, to read one another, in the best conditions. They learn to love each other.

For each exercise, I would distinguish between two levels; the infant stage of the puppy and the precise learning of the adult. With a very young animal, everything is in the fingertips, everything is conveyed in light touches, almost without resorting to physical constraint.

For the adult it is necessary to find the right buttons, that is to say the methods, the particular motivations or the degree of force required to obtain the desired result.

I will limit myself to proposing a small number of solutions. When a problem appears, there is a multitude of ways to resolve it. But it is the nature of the beast that I can never cover one topic in sufficient detail. To deal with walking to heel would take more than a book in its own right.

Each day, the new master can discover a new solution or a new theory. Training is an evolving art. Everyone can make his contribution.

Walking to heel

To get a puppy to walk to heel, choose the induced method. As soon as he comes to your left side of his own accord, tell him, 'Heel, well done!' and stroke him. As I have already said, this is the slowest but the richest method.

You can also put a fine string round his neck, in a more dictatorial method. A length of three or four metres is enough. Then you go on a walk with the string trailing freely on the ground.

About once every ten minutes, you surreptitiously pick up the slack at the end of the cord, and you react with a light jerk, quickly released, when the animal pulls because he is at the limit of his range of action. In the same time, you speak kindly to him, 'It's all right, good dog, come here!'

Japanese Akita Inu

If he comes near, get down and stroke him. If he heads off to the other end of the long line, send him another sequence of jerk-invitation-possibility of being stroked. Everything should take place without putting you out, while you continue walking in the same direction and at the same speed.

Your left hand stays available. Whether it holds the lead or not, its rôle is to stroke the animal whenever it comes into contact with your left leg, whether of its own accord or after a jerk. Congratulate your young pupil verbally whenever he comes near or looks at you.

The quantity of praise should be proportional to his behaviour. If he comes half a centimetre nearer, a simple, 'Well done,' is enough. If he charges towards you, looking for eye contact, he deserves an outburst of ecstasy, 'Yes, you superhero, you Einstein you, that's wonderful, well done!' It is in your interest to hold back a caress for the moment when he is back in complete contact; major effort deserves major reward. The puppy is therefore given a straightforward alternative. Either he belts off to the far end of the long line, and receives an unpleasant jerk, or he approaches his master and receives kind words and caresses. Which do you think he's more likely to choose?

In a few days, you have established good walking to heel. For the young animal, everything happens as if controlled by a mysterious magic force, which always pushes him to be beside his master.

Progressively, reduce his field of action. But this time, before the jerk, insert a moderate warning, 'Easy!' for example.

The day will come when, of his own accord, your puppy won't want to quit the contact of your left leg. Then it will be enough to say, 'Heel!' and as we have already seen, the mechanism of the chain reaction will work.

With an adult, the principle remains the same. Hold the lead, the left hand available at any moment for a caress, then a verbal warning followed by a jerk if the animal pulls the lead, kind words if he doesn't pull and a lovely massage of his right cheek if he puts this in contact with your left leg. All of this while walking, without changing speed or direction. Quite simply, with an older dog, the jerks and the 'warning bells' can be more vigorous.

Be careful not to change direction or pace otherwise your four-footed companion will say to himself, 'OK if I overtake I'll get a pull on my neck but just after that my leader will stop or turn to stroke me, probably to ask for forgiveness; so I can make him stop or turn whenever I like – I just have to overtake him!'

A jerk, even a vigorous one, is not an event. Continue on your way as if nothing has happened. Just stroke your dog when he has decided to glue himself to your knee, or start the jerk routine again, more strongly, if he stays at a distance.

How far away does the dog have the right to go? Everyone

has to decide that for himself. In my view, if the animal goes further away by half a centimetre, that is too far. A dog is truly walking to heel when his right cheek is against my left leg.

Changing Direction

Does the dog really know how to walk to heel correctly, cheek glued to your knee? Imperceptibly, go off at an angle in a movement curving to the right. Perhaps distracted a little, the animal is letting you escape a little? A sharp jerk, with, 'Hey! Are you dreaming or what?' will remind him to pay attention. At the same time as telling him off, tap your left hand loudly against your left thigh so as to refocus the concentration of your absent-minded pupil.

As he already knows how to react to this manual encouragement, he will return almost automatically to stick to your side. Obviously you should make the most of this to lavish physical and verbal caresses on him.

Let's go back to the left hand for a moment; this constitutes the most important tool for this exercise. Always open and available, its function is to deliver affection. When you command, 'Heel!' it is not so that you can demand Prussian-style submission but rather as a reminder, 'Look at my hand, so close to your head; don't forget that if you burrow your nose between my hand and my thigh, there is a caress in it for you. My hand never leaves my thigh? Then little friend, it's up to you to come into contact!'

Watch out for a common mistake; if you stroke the dog at the wrong moment, just when he's about to move away from you, you're telling him how pleased you are when he escapes! How many centimetres can you allow him to move away before you react? None at all.

So, the animal now knows how to stay close during large bends to the right. Move in tighter curves, to the point where you pivot back on yourself, always keeping the quadruped against your left leg.

Next, follow the same progression on bends to the left. You can just as easily alternate right and left from the start. The most difficult action to elicit is the on-the-spot pivot, anti-clockwise. In this exercise, the dog has to keep moving backwards, keeping against your leg all the time.

Before you stop for the first time, slow down for a few steps. At the same time, tell your dog off if he overtakes you, 'Hey, slowly!' By all means, tap your leg to attract his attention, if it wanders for a moment. When you stop, you can decide that the animal has to sit or that he is allowed to remain standing. But don't let him overtake your knee.

To set off again, just start moving forward. The first times, you can resort to words. 'Come on then, little sausage!' Tap your hand against your thigh and jerk on the lead if the dog forgets to move forward with you.

When everything is going well, drop the strap. Let it trail on the ground from now on. The only weapons you have now are your voice and the caress given by your left hand. That is enough to keep the animal beside you. Little by little your confidence will grow.

One day, you will take off the collar and lead and your dog will walk beside you, glued like a limpet to your knee. That day, you can raise a glass to celebrate!

In town, either to keep to the municipal regulations or because the dog is no longer showing perfect obedience, attach the lead once more. A little revision from time to time never does any harm.

When you are completely sure of yourself, move up to senior school; walking to heel, no lead, moving backwards either in a straight line or turning. At this level, everyone can easily invent his own programme.

Sit

Nothing is easier than to make a puppy sit. Using the induction method, order, 'Sit!' when he is sitting. Over time, this method functions like a dream.

Using a method with more constraint, press gently down on his rump while repeating, 'Sit!' Make the young animal put his posterior on the ground. And watch for the slightest sign of submission.

If, while you are pressing his rump down, the puppy finishes the motion of his own accord and sits, stop forcing him. Praise him. When he gives in, you give in. Follow his action, let him be obedient. And congratulate him again when he is sitting.

In this way, very quickly, he will lower his hind-quarters the moment he hears the command, 'Sit!', or as soon as he sees your hand moving towards his back. One day, he will obey the simple sound of your voice.

Remember that it is necessary, at first anyway, to pronounce the word, 'Sit!' with exactly the same intonation each time, for example emphasising the 't', in 'SiT', or hissing the 'Sssit!'.

Is he starting to sit? 'Good dog, sit!' It's better not to use his name because that might make think it's a recall and stop him half-way. After a few days, add in a caress on his forehead. He gets up before he's allowed? No punishment. The time of 'Sit and stay' has not arrived yet. For the moment, try and have only good associations between the dog's actions and the words you use for them. Very soon you will begin to capture his attention. The animal sits when you say 'Sit!'. For he knows now that afterwards he'll get a 'Well done!' and a caress.

Be careful; at this stage you shouldn't use 'Sit!' or 'Down' as punishments, like putting the dog in a corner. Obedience is too precious to be wrecked.

If this first approach is not enough, move on to the enticement phase. Fix the lead to some system of hook fixed on the ground, leaving little slack so that the animal can't jump in the air or get up, and attach the lead connection to the dog's collar. Next, put a few treats down, just in front of the dog. At the moment that your hand dives over his head, he is going to look up towards the sky. As the lead holds him back, he is either going to become mad with anger, in which case you leave him – the punishment for being off-side in this game is that the dog is left alone – or he will sit nicely. At that moment, put in a 'Well done, sit!'

If he's a rebel, you have to resort to some constraint. But beware alpha dogs. They frequently oppose your intervention with all their might. By its nature, the dog tends to push when you pull him and pull when you push him. Humans too, so …

Before using brute strength, restrain yourself to gently putting to work simple physical guidance. Get down on your knees facing the animal's right hand side, gently slip your right hand around his neck, slip your right hand under his neck, in his collar, so as to keep him in place, then say, 'Good dog, sit!' And press gently with a slice of your left hand against the back of his rear knees as if you're cutting his knee-caps. He will react be moving away from this contact behind his legs, folding them; he is sitting! Once he's sitting, 'Well done, good dog!'

When this action is established, work to hold the command. The animal isn't allowed to change position unless you have given the release command, or 'Go and play' or of course the command to do something different.

With a recalcitrant adult, the method stays the same. But you are reduced to using a higher degree of physical force. Double the effect on the rear by a light jerk of the collar upwards. Be careful, once again, to stop all constraint instantly at the first sign of good intentions.

Down

The reader who has understood how to obtain a 'Sit' already knows how to demand 'Down'. The film rolls in the same way, just as well for a puppy as an adult, but, this time, the elbows and backs of knees should rest on the ground. The ideal position is that known as the 'sphinx', but if the animal lies down 'cow fashion', flanks and elbows on the ground, the dog is more stationary. Distance yourself. He should, without suffering, hold this position for several hours.

Staying down is not hard work. 'Down! Stay!' holds a privileged position in dog-training. With very little expenditure of energy, it is the perfect way to establish your dominant status as master.

It is enough just to keep an eye on your dog, which should stay down until given the release command.

At the slightest movement of your pupil, go back towards him murmuring words of displeasure; 'You good-for-nothing, you think I'm joking do you? That won't do at all, will it now.' Don't repeat the command or you lose face. In this way you let the animal know straight away that he is about to annoy you.

If he lies down again, of his own accord, when you walk

towards him, tell him, 'That's better. I'm much happier when you do that!' then move back again.

If the dog stays on his feet, go right up to him, put him back in the same spot, in his original position, facing the same direction, exactly where he lay down in the first place. At each return, after disobedience restrain him a little more strongly, following the principle of escalation. At some point, he will stop rebelling. you will have found the level of coercion that is effective. And, of course, you will do everything to lower this threshold to its lightest, in the sessions that follow.

Good masters will disappear and re-appear from a hiding-place. The dog thinks they're a long way away. Surprise! Who is there behind the tree, telling him off? Daddy!

At first, to make sure that the animal doesn't head for the hills when you go away, attach him to a stake or a nearby fence, with a long line. If he gets up, at least you'll be able to find him straight away. He can't disappear.

He should keep the same position despite any distraction. You come back, you caress him, you shout at him how good-looking he is? He should stay down. An empty jam-jar lands beside his head, a lion comes sniffing him, a bitch on heat flaunts her attractions? He should stay down.

He is not allowed to get up until you have given a counter-order or the release command.

With this regime, your pupil learns to submit. The 'down' can take place on a pavement or in an empty bath, or under a railway bridge with a train going overhead. All these exercises toughen up the dog, teaching him to keep his cool and to trust his master.

Be careful all the same to protect your pupil from any danger. One day I made my dog Victor go down in the middle of the car park at the training club in St-Lô. His life was only saved thanks to lookers-on who shouted a warning; someone manoeuvring a car was just about to reverse towards this obedient animal. The vehicle stopped thirty centimetres away from him and he hadn't moved at all!

There is no such thing as an intelligent accident.

The recall

The fourth pillar of a basic education, recall, has already been well prepared by the exercise of walking to heel. In practice, this is actually a permanent recall from nearby. To obtain good recall, clean and at a gallop, you need nothing more than the fine string when you set off. Let it trail on the ground. At one moment or another, the dog is going to head off to amuse himself. You are not far away so pick up the string and, at the moment the animal starts to pull it taut, call him, 'Prince, come here!'

There are two possible reactions; either he turns round and heads back, in which case, praise him, or he carries on and inflicts a backwards jerk on himself, all the stronger the more quickly he's moving away. As for your part, if you think it necessary, you can always pull the string more sharply backwards. Obviously you should limit yourself to very restrained jerks.

With an adult dog, nothing stops you acting with great determination. After the jerk, you will again meet with two types of reaction; either the dog will carry on escaping or he will start to return. In the first case, send a new, stronger jerk along the line, according to the principle of escalation. In the second, crouch down, encourage him verbally to continue his return, open your arms in welcome and smile. To speed up his return, clap him loudly, repeating 'Well done, that's great my super-genius!' in vibrant tones.

While the animal is coming towards you, don't go to meet him. Right to the last moment, it's up to him to make the contact. Keep your hands against your body. He will have his caress, for sure, but only when he has earned it, when he is touching you.

At that precise moment, you should explode with joy. The reward should be enormous, like a fireworks display of compliments, caresses and fun. At first, you can add in treats. Your pupil makes a run for it at the last minute? He's inviting you to play. Don't have any of it. Step back in the opposite direction to him. If necessary, pivot so that you are once more, always, facing him while continuing to move backwards and speaking kindly to him. If you have to, give one last jerk to help you obtain the contact.

During the return, drop the string. But, at the slightest slowing down, or if the dog looks like escaping, pick it up again to give a little jerk in punishment.

Then, as time goes by, put in the recall command at any moment during a walk, sometimes at twenty metres, sometimes at two, sometimes at eight. Clearly you want to be able to do without the string, little by little.

During the first lessons, don't allow your dog to go off without the string. When you take him somewhere, a public park for instance, where other masters let their dogs loose each day, he is going to charge off after a little friend one day or another. Don't panic; you have to hand a method of control. And, if you have dropped the string, head nonchalantly not towards the dog but towards the end of the string. When you've caught it, you've caught your dog!

In his head, your dog ends up taking note of your amazing powers. Usually, he gives in pretty quickly.

One last detail; on a daily walk, you can settle for an approximate recall. Let the animal patrol a little in front of you, whistle or send a discreet, 'Pssst!' then head off in the opposite direction to that which you have been following to date. When the dog comes back, tell him, 'Good dog!' but without going into transports of joy, and don't react if he moves away again.

This message signifies, 'Pssst, I'm changing direction, so if you don't want to lose me, stay in the vicinity.' But don't demand perfect walking to heel all the time. Know how to accept a little imprecision when the finest obedience isn't essential.

Picardy Shepherd Dog

CHAPTER 8

The re-education of a difficult dog

'Everything is difficult before it is easy'

THOMAS FULLER

Angel and demon at the same time, the dog, former wolf, is permanently torn between two contradictory impulses;

1. The absolute obligation to obey the leader, the 'alpha', essential for the survival of the pack because a wolf doesn't know how to hunt effectively solo.
2. The need to challenge the leader of the pack, to make sure the latter is always the best, physically and mentally. Among wolves, a king who is failing, ill or wounded is unthinkable – he would be yesterday's news within seconds!

As a consequence, your wolf-heir will obey you and challenge you all at once, and constantly. It's up to you to behave like a

Weimaraner

pack leader on top form. You should be aware that the best lead and the best book in the world won't produce any results if you don't put some work in on yourself. Do you want your difficult dog to change his behaviour? Change your own first! For the dog is always adapting his ways to those of the people around him.

This continual adaptation turns out to be very valuable and offers remedies for even the worst faults, ensuring that a dog's behaviour is not set in concrete forever. There is always a way to modify behaviour, whatever the age, background and character of the animal.

To achieve this result, the most important factor is to really want it. And to learn the rules of the game.

In the same way that they have studied normal learning, dog psychologists have tried to bring to light the principles that rule the re-establishment of good habits, some form of re-training.

Everyone thinks first of punishment when a dog does something wrong. This topic could have a book all to itself. It's not that I'm writing off this method completely but I am convinced that in the saying, 'Who loves well, punishes well', 'well' does not mean 'frequently'.

Some truths are worth repeating:-

- Every weapon wears out, so shouldn't be used too often.
- A good master uses the exact minimum of punishment required.
- Don't resort to punishment when you've lost your temper.
- Never hit your dog.

In practice, punishment works a bit like the steering-wheel on a car. The tool's simple appearance hides great sophistication. You think you know everything by instinct but when you first learn to drive a vehicle, you are surprised by phenomena you hadn't predicted.

Dog-trainers know that an unsuitable, badly handled punishment, far from calming and curing an aggressive dog, is likely to render it even more dangerous.

At best it merely displaces the problem; if a dog that barks all the time is hit as a punishment, he might start destroying the apartment instead. The most inconvenient thing about punishment is that it teaches the animal nothing, least of all what he should have done. Punishment is limited in meaning to, 'That's not good,' with regard to a past event which the animal might or might not remember.

For these reasons, you shouldn't use punishment without trying one of the following solutions first.

The process of re-education

Extinguishing unwanted behaviour

This occurs when the animal stops carrying out certain actions for lack of appropriate reinforcement. When you want to practise this process of extinguishing a dog's bad behaviour, the difficulty is that you first have to work out all the reinforcements that are sustaining the behaviour.

Let's take the situation of a dog that wants to sleep on a couch where his master doesn't want him to be. Why does she choose this one place rather than another? Perhaps because, from time to time, tired of fighting, the master, while comfortably sitting on the couch, lets him climb up beside him and gives him some pleasant caresses. Perhaps the dog considers it to be a comfortable warm bed for the night to come. Perhaps he has occasionally discovered cake crumbs buried in the cushions. The couch has become a sort of island of dreams! It is up to you to work out what exactly is the reinforcement of the dog's longing to pass the long nights on the couch. Then you have to arrange things so he no longer finds any satisfaction there. From now on, no-one nibbles so much as a peanut there, no-one gives him a cuddle there. And, furthermore, pour icy liquid all over the couch before leaving the room. As you see, extinguishing bad behaviour is not a simple technique.

If you have worked out the reinforcements which come together to perpetuate an undesirable habit, cut off all the sources that feed it. This should be enough. But, sometimes, you realise that, far from disappearing, quite the contrary, the behaviour has become more frequent. We call this phenomenon, 'The extinguishing explosion'. Everything takes place as if, on the point of being extinguished, the habit has had a new lease of life. It is imperative that you continue your efforts, without weakening. If you give up now, you will have far more difficulties in the future in reaching the desire result, as the bad habit will have take an even stronger hold.

On the other hand, if you keep up every effort, you will rapidly see the light at the end of tunnel. The undesirable habit will disappear little by little, even if you see occasional lapses, what we call, 'spontaneous recurrences'. You're complaining about the painful length of this method? Turning a deaf ear to the insistant demand of a dog determined to come and sit on the forbidden couch, can play havoc with the strongest nerves. But the game is worth the candle. By resorting to the technique of extinguishing bad behaviour, you haven't had to use punishment.

Substitution

Replace unwanted behaviour with desirable actions. For example, before telling off a dog that barks madly when a strange rings the doorbell, ask him to lie down in his basket; if he obeys, just as you want, reward him. In this way, you're moving from a system of punishment to instructions and rewards, associated with teaching a good action!

Counter-conditioning

As its name indicates, it calls on the principles of Pavlov (classic conditioning) and on those of Thorndike (operant conditioning), but it functions inversely to received habits.

Suppose, for instance, that your bullmastiff barks himself silly when he sees the postman approach the garden fence. His behaviour is becoming extreme and you are starting to worry.

In fact the animal has developed a conditioned reflex:-

1. The postman arrives
2. 'I'll frighten him by barking.'
3. 'That made him go away. I've won!'

If, one fine day, you decide to stop this undesirable behaviour, you can imagine some counter-conditioning. As soon as someone comes near the fence, accept a few barks – your guardian is doing his job – then make him go to his corner and stay there. After that, you can let your visitor in.

The first sessions take place on a lead, using the lightest possible constraint. Little by little, you will be able to use just your voice to send the dog to his corner.

The day will come when the animal will go and lie down in his bed when the doorbell rings. He will have internalised the counter-conditioning which has now cured his bad habits.

The result depends on your determination, and also on some carefully chosen rewards; for example a piece of cheese that your dog finds in his den, as if by chance, the moment he arrives there.

Predict and plan calmly how these sessions of counter-conditioning will unfold. Call on your friends. Ask them to ring the doorbell at a time agreed beforehand, warning them that you won't open to them straight away. All the actors will therefore be prepared for the scene.

Alaskan Malamute

Similar to the technique of substitution, counter-conditioning comes down to replacing one reflex action with another. Here again, it is important to bring enough determination and perseverance to bear on the problem. Unless you want to become what Mao Tse Tung would have called a 'paper tiger', never considered by the dog as worthy of respect.

Desensitisation

The practice of desensitisation is very much like the treatment against allergies. First you determine what agent produces the reaction, then you teach the organism to get used to it very gradually.

Let's take the case of the hunting dog that's afraid of a gun-shot. First you put him somewhere he feels totally secure, in the crook of his master's arms, for instance. Then, at a distance, someone bursts a paper bag that has been filled with air, at a moment when the master is talking calmly to his young pupil and giving him a big cuddle. Progressively, as days go by, the bag-bursting gets closer and closer. If you take the precaution of withdrawing at the least hint of fear in the young animal, and starting the operation all over again from the point where there was no reaction, success is guaranteed over time.

You can speed up the process if you associate desensitisation with counter-conditioning. So, in the case of the puppy fright-ened by the noise of the vacuum-cleaner, the cure is more rapid if you demonstrate to the animal that the noise of the vacuum-cleaner automatically precedes the arrival of a piece of cheese from his master's hand. For the dog, this noise, previously terri-fying, becomes little by little an interesting signal, announcing pleasure.

Immersion

If this has the same objectives as desensitisation, that is to say showing the animal that there is nothing to fear, immersion acts with much greater brutality.

Everyone has heard of the swimming instructors who throw their pupils in the swimming pool to show that fear of water has no foundation, Sometimes this works, if the swimming instructor has done his work well beforehand, if he has taught the tech-nique of swimming properly to the student he has pushed in the water, if the student can swim even if he doesn't believe he can. But this method can also result in a catastrophe. Immersion should therefore be practised in a discriminating way.

The principle consists of immersing the dog in his problem, then preventing him from running away so that he ends up by accepting the situation and digging deep into his own resources to face the challenge.

Keeping to the example of the hunting dog that's scared of gunshot, you could attach him to a short, strong chain and let loose all kinds of explosions around him (bursts of bangers, gunshots, the crack of a pistol). At first, the terrified animal will struggle furiously. Little by little, he will calm down. At that moment, you can stop the noise, when the dog shows he can bear the explosions, and so at the moment when he is less afraid.

The disadvantage of this rather brutal method is that it can drag out a high level of anxiety for a long time. It's true that, generally, an organism gets used to anything in time, but you should always remember the exceptions. That same organism might just decide it's had enough. It has actually happened that dogs have died of fear. Immersion, reserved for the most serious problems, should always be used with the greatest caution.

In practice, I never use it. I prefer to make progress slowly. I would always use gradual habituation.

Habituation

In a way, this is a kind version of immersion. It consists of putting the animal frequently in the environments which scare him a little – streets or shop entrances for instance – and then waiting until he gets used to them. One essential factor; the master must keep in contact with his dog. Common sense dictates that you have to stop the animal running away and also be on hand for reassurance.

The tool of choice for this is always the lead, attached to a collar. On the lead the dog can't evade whatever treatment you want him to experience, and you can get close to him to caress him.

The difficult dog

Let's establish right from the start that this animal, the bête noir of insurance companies dealing with civic responsibilities, does not suffer from health problems. A thorough veterinary check is therefore essential. It might reveal unexpected afflictions. A dog that urinates all over an apartment could be suffering from cystitis. If a dog bites every hand that touches him, it's always possible that his retina is in the process of atrophying. He is becoming blind and so fears all these vague shapes that approach him. If the difficult dog is in good health, then this is a dog which hasn't learned to respect his owner. We can distinguish two large categories; the less dangerous and the very dangerous.

Basenji

The less dangerous

There is a whole range of bizarre behaviours; he barks madly without stopping, he destroys everything in the house, or prevents husband from joining wife in the conjugal bed between three and four o'clock in the morning... Some dogs specialise in chasing chickens. Ah, let us contemplate for a moment all those good fowl, savagely cut down in the flower of their youth, by our baby wolves!

From now on, even when you really want to cuddle your loony dog, start by prescribing him a regime of 'Nothing comes for free any more!'

The preceding dialogue went something like this:-

Master: 'Now then, I really want to cuddle him, this good-for-nothing, because I love him despite his awful personality. And anyway, he looks at me with so much longing!'

Dog: 'Now then, my slave gave me something to eat when I nipped his foot and growled. Now he's coming to see me to ask forgiveness for his inadequacies. I shall be an indulgent prince and accept his gestures of submission.

I'll lie on my back just to show I'm not in the least scared of him. Ohhhh, that's nice. OK, that's enough now, I'll just give him a little bite to make him stop.'

Master: 'Ow! The little devil has bitten me again. Too bad for him, I'll stop stroking him. Or perhaps I haven't stroked him enough – it's true, I've been neglecting him, poor little thing…'

Result; the dog will bite again to get more caresses and the master will fall for it; 'He's a good dog at heart, all the same, and he has lovely eyes…'

From now on, the rôles are reversed. 'I want to stroke him. But first, I'm going to make him follow a command. 'Come here!' or any other command will do, 'Sit!' for example, if he's already lying down. It's meal-time? First I'm going to order him 'Down!' or 'Bark!' or 'Give me your paw!', whatever, any command, but a command, which he has to obey.

Don't use the same command too often, or the animal will take the upper hand by anticipating it. 'I'm going to lie down before your command, just to show you that I don't give a fig about you, and I've noticed that obeying before the command really winds you up and takes away all your weapons, so now, slave, give me my food right away!'

Beware the dog's mental mechanisms! Remember the true story of Pavlov's dog; 'I know how to get my master to ring the bell. All I have to do is drool…'

The very dangerous

He has already bitten several members of the family, or strangers. What can you do about such a big problem?

Most of the time, it is because of the human being's good intentions that the dog has become a domestic tyrant. The most common fault is the little tap, either with a hand or with a rolled newspaper.

Some veterinary surgeons advocate various pharmaceutical remedies, or castration, to calm a very dangerous dog down. But as it's a question of absence of a hierarchical order, in the vast majority of cases, and not of a medical problem, the intervention of the man in green, doesn't always have a sustained impact. You can, of course, keep your dog half-asleep on drugs all the rest of his life, but to what good? Most of the time, a competent dog-trainer can resolve the difficulty without resorting to strong chemicals.

Personally, I approach the re-training of a very dangerous dog with two convictions:-

- In the heart of every breed, you will find killer beasts.
- You can always reclaim the dog on condition that you re-create the hierarchical order that is missing; unless you're dealing with the extremely rare case of a mentally ill dog.

Every dog has his own talents, whether these are developed or latent. Within sensible limits, everything is possible. Calming down a biter included.

In the high valleys of Tibet, with the terrifying mastiffs of the mountains, just as in the protection dogs' competition rings with Belgian Shepherd Dogs, trainers prove that they can really control animals with extremely strong personalities. Tibetan mastiffs or Belgian Shepherd Dogs from working lines are actually animals selected according to their bite and their instinct to do so. Nevertheless they present no problems of behaviour, because their masters know how to hold them back appropriately, according to the occasion.

In the case of a domestic dog calling the tune for everyone in his world, it is useful to determine the origins of the situation first. Most of the time, you believed you were doing the right thing in accepting, initially, to bend over backwards to satisfy the animal's whims.

Did he want to climb on the couch? You squeezed up to make room for him. Did he growl his displeasure when you clumsily sat on the end of his paw? You thought it plain good manners to say sorry and respect his comfort by moving a little further away. Besides, he came so quickly to ask forgiveness, rolling on his back, with such a repentant look, that you stroked him straight away, full of affection. You even played with him and let him chew on your fist. Without realising it, you taught your dog to make unrestrained use of his teeth.

It was funny, touching even, this little defenseless creature playing the villain. Even today, when he growls or barks at people who approach you, you ask him in a gentle voice to calm down. You even stroke him, hoping to calm him down and quieten him. Acting in this way, you achieve one sole result. You demonstrate to him how pleased you are when he menaces passers-by. He barks, you congratulate him. What exactly do you think you're training him to do?

In fact, you're preparing this dog to be a real killer. With the best intentions, you are manufacturing a hell that you won't escape from without help. If you accept obedience to this little wolf, hierarchical milestones will ambush you all the time. When he is there, tummy in the air, demanding the caress due to the top dog, you will lose face. You will end up afraid of his growling. Sooner or later, you will also be afraid of his curling lip and unsheathed fangs.

Emergency solutions

The re-training of a dangerous dog is essentially the same as that of a non-dangerous one, but I advocate the use of an emergency solution right from the start; totally eradicate any chance of your dog biting, thanks to a mechanical device. For this, I rely on two accessories, the Shellclip muzzle and the magicol. (See the Doggbagy catalogue on www.dogmasters.com)

Next, we have to activate the 'relocation syndrome', a psychological shock thanks to which you can reset the clocks to the hour. Whether the dog is very dangerous or just a little, start working with determination on the three basic exercises – recall, walking to heel and the down-stay – that is to say, close control, control from a distance and control of the two together, so as to convince the animal that he is not leader of the pack. This will be more difficult than with a 3 month old puppy, but just remind yourself, the dog beyond redemption is almost non-existent.

It will sometimes be necessary to come to a physical confrontation, mammal against mammal, to a sort of strong-arm contest, to get back to a clear and sustainable surrender from the animal. One good immobilisation is enough, held until the moment when the dog calms down.

Don't trust harmful advice; the canine psychologist, Benjamin Hart, asserts that you should not be afraid to inflict on the dog suffering identical to that he intended for you. I do not agree; can you really imagine yourself biting your dog in the thigh because he took a chunk out of your buttock? In my view, it is enough to show the animal systematically that he loses every confrontation between him and me.

Set the right scene by behaving in the same way as with a normal dog, but increasing the intensity of your rewards and punishments.

Great Dane (Harlequin)

Unfortunately, the owner of a dangerous dog doesn't have the leeway, the sang-froid or the technique to take his difficult pupil in hand. If he doesn't feel he has the competence or the heart to take on the enterprise of setting the dog back on the right path himself, despite all his willingness, then he can always entrust the re-education of his dog to a specialist. As far as I'm concerned, I operate a re-training strategy with two strands.

I work with the dog myself because I believe that it is up to me, the specialist, to take the dog back in hand. Then, when the animal understands – sometimes for the first time in his life – that he has truly come across someone who is not at all impressed, who knows how to demand and obtain obedience, then the boot's on the other foot.

The re-training scenario

It takes about two to six hours to get to know the animal's personality, plus those of his owners, to note the detail of the problems and then to establish a solid re-training. I prefer that the owners are present; that way, they can see for themselves how difficult things are, and observe that there are no blows or medication, just rapid changes in the behaviour of their animal.

By the simple fact of turning the hierarchy the other way up – in favour of the human this time – weird problems disappear first, as if by magic. By 'weird' problems, I mean problems that are very easily resolved; excessive barking, destruction, escapes, nerves in the car, for example, which respond to simple strategies. Clearly, for the owners, these are not in any way irrelevant problems… But they are so easy to sort out that, sometimes, it's not even worth me charging for the lesson.

The results are even better if the re-training takes place in the territory that the animal feels most confident, that is to say in his usual environment, his home. Only there can I detect what I have christened 'cursed corners', those places where, because he has been bitten there already, the master dare not put his hand if the dog's hiding out there, places such as underneath furniture or various hidey-holes. In these places, the dog has the conviction that he cannot be touched or punished by his owner. He has acquired the certainty that his power there is without limits.

Behavioural problems disappear the day the dog admits that he is not the leader of the pack and that, from now on, nothing counts for more than the commands of his master. His brain is now so busy with this that he has no time to misbehave. The quality of re-training dictates the cure; badly done, re-education reinforces the animal's conviction that man is just a paper tiger.

Important point; never comfort, praise or stroke a difficult dog in the ten seconds or less following a punishment, even if he at last deigns to obey you. If you ignore this rule, you will activate the following paradoxical association:-

1. 'I do something bad and my master punishes me.'
2. 'Just afterwards, he strokes me.'
3. 'Therefore, if I want to be stroked, I need to do something really bad!'

You are sparking off a sort of canine version of the famous syllogism; a rare horse is expensive, a one-eyed horse is rare, so a one-eyed horse is expensive.

The second strand of my strategy is to undertake the apprenticeship of the owner. Don't believe those who repeat the stupid remark, 'A dog can only obey one master'. If that were true, I would have lost all my clients donkeys' years ago. The truth is far simpler; the dog obeys everyone who knows the right codes and uses them!

After having shown the owner how things are done, I put the lead in his hand and I teach him how to carry on from where I left off. This time, the bold quadruped co-operates; his two masters are right beside him and behaving in the same way.

Without this phase of apprenticeship for the owner, all retraining is an illusion. With it, little by little, the master becomes completely autonomous. This takes time. Just as much as his dog, he needs to become familiar with new gestures and new concepts of authority.

It is possible to sweeten the bad character of a dangerous dog, but it is also possible to rebuild the confidence of a timid animal. The objective is exactly the same for a fearful creature; the dog has to obey a command, whatever happens, even in the midst of events that frighten him. When his brain is busy, he doesn't have time to be frightened!

The owner at last becomes a master and follows up by creating situations where the animal gradually toughens up in a good way and learns not to worry any more.

It would be an illusion to pretend to resolve all the possible, conceivable problems presented by dogs, in a book. When bad habits have been established, sometimes over many years, I say again that only the intervention of a competent trainer is capable of putting the dog and his owner back on the right road.

Long live mistakes!

Once your difficulties are largely resolved, harden up the four variables of learning, my famous four Ds; ' duration, distance, distraction and difficulty'.

For each of the basic exercises – heel, down-stay, recall – increase the duration, the distance between you and the dog, the distractions and the difficulties, but gradually. Don't hesitate to take a step back if the pupil can't meet the challenge. Once again, it is up to each person to create his own solutions, with the understanding that it is unacceptable to work an animal that is tired or that doesn't have the technical knowledge required to work at the level demanded.

Following all this, for all dogs, whether dangerous or not, there comes a time to verify what has been learned. Then you can proceed to the moment of truth; provoke the animal to make a mistake. Without this phase, you will never have total confidence either in yourself or in your dog. In training, I demand 300% obedience from my dog so that I can hope for 100% for a day in the ring.

Let's take the example of an animal that's difficult to recall. You have succeeded with a moderately good recall but you are still not sure how reliable this is.

Attach a long line to your pupil's collar, then take him somewhere you think he will probably refuse to come when he's called, in a public park where there are other dogs, for example. Go near to an animal that seems to you to be particularly playful. Inevitably, your dog will hurtle towards the other dog. Take the opportunity to give a command, in a light tone, 'Bobby, here!'

If, having learned from previous experiences, your dog comes to you, belly low on the ground, rain compliments and a thousand encouragements on him. Perhaps, on the contrary, he turns a deaf ear? In that case, a good shake of the lead will remind him of his duty.

Pushing a dog to make a mistake so that you can correct him, when he didn't really want to make a mistake, is like tapping the couch for him to climb up then telling him forcibly, 'No, you can't climb up' once he finally tries to do so. After several repetitions of this manoeuvre, he will hate the damned couch. He won't even want to put his paws or his forehead on it ever again.

A mistake constitutes the tool to choose when you want to firm up some solid learning. The setbacks of today always pave the way for the successes of tomorrow.

The point is that you don't need to worry when your pupil is tempted to a little peccadillo. Calmly, without getting agitated, explain to him simply that you are not pleased. If you have carried out the first lessons properly, the animal will understand perfectly the difference between 'Yes!' and 'No!', between 'That's a good, good Basil-dog!' murmured in a warm, thrilled voice, and 'Hmmm, what exactly are you up to then, oh no, I don't think so my little friend, do you take me for an idiot or what!' delivered in the cadences of displeasure tinged with menace.

When the dog makes a mistake, start off the escalation of constraint from the lowest possible degree. Or even stop everything and put the animal straight away in his corner. Ignore him for a whole day, using the famous theory of the cold shoulder. After this, try once more the exercise he got wrong, and give him the chance to redeem himself.

If he carries on getting it wrong, continue with the same treatment. The dog has to learn that his master is more stubborn than he is, and that the master has a few more tricks up his sleeve.

If need be, invent your own tactics. But don't give up and don't give in to brutality either. You would be handing victory on a plate to your obstinate opponent. The only effect would be to harden him in his rebuttals.

When you have put right the behaviour of your dog, stay vigilant. The animal will always be at risk of a relapse, of a resurgence of the old behaviour. However, as you will notice, these relapses are less and less serious and less and less frequent if you don't put up with them. From now on, everything depends on your determination and your perseverance. I can't stand in for you in your own home!

And if, driven to despair, you can't find any manoeuvre capable of changing the animal's behaviour, call once more on a competent dog-trainer. Each to his own profession!

Choosing a trainer

Another source of information is direct advice in the field from a competent trainer.

There are clubs, well established in many countries. Unfortunately the great dog-trainers there are difficult to approach. They already lack the time they would wish to work with their own dogs, so they're not going to lose even more time with beginners. So you will probably turn to those professionals who dedicate their lives, not to shining in competitions but to their clients. Choose one who guarantees his work for the whole life of the dog, without asking any supplementary payment for revision sessions, and who accepts that you are with him from start to finish.

Pyrenean Mountain Dog

The quantity and arguments of publicity posters are not necessarily synonymous with quality of training. Before trusting your animal, make some enquiries. Does your trainer guarantee as many revision lessons as you need? Will he make you pay for extra lessons if he hasn't succeeded in training your dog first time round? Does he work in the open, with you beside him, or does he take your dog alone, without witnesses, behind a clump of trees? Does he get rapid results? All the trainers in our team, as detailed on dogmasters.com, possess the necessary savoir-faire that I'm describing. Some money-making trainers have a neat way of passing the buck when there's a setback; they claim that it's the dog's fault, because he has a bad personality, or that the master doesn't understand a thing, or doesn't know how to take on board the training, or, best of all, that it's the fault of the breeder in selling a dog that can't be trained!

But it's exactly for this reason that the master goes to see the trainer, to learn. If the trainer doesn't have the technical skills himself, he can't teach them to others, and most certainly not to the dog! If you make a mistake the first time you choose a trainer, go and see another one. Long live mistakes, among humans too!

CHAPTER 9

Everyday problems

'Every problem resolved gives birth to others, generally more difficult,'

GEORGES POMPIDOU

Some difficulties lie in wait for just about every master. Here are some effective methods for dealing with the most common problems.

The mad barker

First of all, have no faith in the operation that consists of cutting his vocal chords!

There are a variety of systems commercially available, electrical or chemical, intended to stop the dog from barking too much. In 1986, I invented the magicol, inspired by the tie-muzzles used by veterinary surgeons and by the muzzle used in the past by the SNCF, the French Railway System. With extraordinary simplicity, it functions without any mechanism or electricity or breakdown. Thousands of satisfied clients and hundreds of dogs saved from being abandoned (people are sorely tempted to part with an animal that barks too much, because of neighbours' complaints).

How to use one; when the dog barks, tell him off, 'Oh no, no, no, oh, no, no, no!' without shouting. At the same time, put the magicol in place. Wait for the animal to calm down before taking it off. That moment could come very quickly. Each time the animal barks, go close to him, making it very clear that you are holding the magicol, shaking it along its length and saying, 'Oh no, no, no, oh, no, no!' Put the magicol on him, then take it off, once more when he has calmed down again. Generally, dogs end up wanting to dive into the first mouse-hole they can find and swallow their barks as soon as they see the master shake the magicol!

In a very short time, perhaps two repetitions for the most malleable dogs, the problem of constant, idiotic barking has disappeared. Without shouting at your dog or hitting him. For some animals, it takes longer.

Be careful – this accessory is not intended to stay on the animal's muzzle long-term. It should be considered as a tool to aid learning, as indispensable as a collar and lead, and is available direct from dogmasters.com

The dog that barks endlessly during the night represents a particular example. Generally, he is barking to get into your bedroom or to get out of the room in which he has been shut. The solution is simple. It comes via the door. Open the door sharply on the dog, just a little. He will be right beside it and it will knock him. After a few repetitions, he'll move backwards when you open the door. At that moment, you will have won, in the short-term at least. Start all over again as many times as is necessary. Little by little act with more vigour. The whole business won't entertain him for very long.

If the door opens towards you, start to open it and then close it again with the same sharpness, just when he's starting to cross the threshold. Be careful; you don't want to crush his head in the doorway! It is always important to keep some judicious moderation when using force with a dog.

There are various devices nowadays which use electricity. Whether they squirt an icy gas or lemon scent or give an electric shock, they function more or less successfully. The concept doesn't thrill me but I have to admit that the ultimate weapon against barking in the master's absence, is the electric collar. You have to choose a model that is effective. Here again, quality determines everything.

The destructive dog

As preventive security, fit a good muzzle on him. When he has lost the habit of biting everything that moves, and everything that stays still, when he has found other sources of interest in his life, then he won't need it any more. It is better to muzzle your treasured dog right away, rather than give him a welt in anger when you find he has destroyed your curtains or carpet.

Unfortunately, classic leather or fabric muzzles all share the same design faults; they hold the dog's muzzle too tightly closed, damage your hands with their sharp fastenings, accumulate bacteria and provoke several allergies. In short, the dog can't put up with one for very long.

Another factor for me was that I often train huskies that work in a pack, and which, because they are always spoiling for a fight, are disqualified from teams despite their exceptional sporting talents.

For all of these reasons, I created the Shellclip muzzle in 1989. It took me two years of adjustments to get the four different sizes just right; cocker spaniel, sheepdog, rottweiler and Great Dane. Originally designed for working dogs, this has nevertheless been adopted by thousands of masters for all sorts of breeds.

Light, well-aired, rot-resistant because it's made from polypropylene, extremely solid, reparable, machine-washable, it allows a dog to open his mouth, to carry out vigorous physical exercise, to drink and even to eat. A real teaching aid, it teaches the dog to control himself. Shellclip muzzles are available from dogmasters.com.

Of course, with a muzzle, the problem is merely camouflaged, not resolved. Only careful re-education can root out the problem. But the result is there; instantly, the dog is unable to cause destruction any more.

House-training

You would like your new companion to learn clean habits rapidly, to ask to go outside when he feels a burning need, and to hold it in when you aren't there? Then, go back a bit, to the stage when the puppy learned, from its mother, not to foul the nest.

Just after birth, the mother energetically licks each little one. The passage of the maternal tongue under the base of the tail releases the flow of urine, and defecation, that she swallows straight away. This is why, in early infancy, when they suckle their mother, when all their intake comes from her teats, the little ones are clean. Only the female deposits her waste products. She goes away from the house and carefully buries her output. The idea, for her, is to give off the slightest possible trace of a scent, so as not to attract the predators, bears or badgers, which feast on small puppies. The little ones are therefore accustomed to growing up in an environment without urine or excrement. This cleanliness determines the survival of the species. Their nest is a little hole dug out at the foot of a tree or under a rock. In this limited space, urine, changing into ammonia, would asphyxiate the babies.

English Cocker Spaniel

Little by little, the puppies start to eat adult food. Then the mother doesn't clean up their output. When they know how to walk, she forbids them to soil the ground. She takes them by the scruff of their neck and packs them off to the door if they assume the position that precedes voiding. They learn to respect the little family nest.

In the natural environment, the dog is therefore clean. But man, with his big boots, generally works hard to destroy this good behaviour. The breeder shuts up puppies in a pen. The animals are therefore forced to break the ancestral law because, quite simply, they can't get out.

Let's return to the mechanism of innate cleanliness. Deal with this question by pressing the buttons of instinctive impulses, of natural mental mechanisms. You can easily and with no danger imitate the behaviour of the bitch. If you have acquired your puppy just before a holiday period or even before an entire weekend, give him all your attention for at least two full days.

Keep him in view for this period. Except of course when he's flat out asleep! As soon as he crouches to urinate, carry him quickly to the lawn or the gutter. Don't interrupt him with ill-timed congratulations that are likely to distract him. When he has finished, take him back inside.

If, instead, he heads of his own accord for the door, open it for him. Don't take any risks. If your dog approaches the door ten times that morning, open it for him ten times and take him out ten times.

Don't raise your voice if, by chance, your dog urinates on your carpet. If you get carried away, you spoil the understanding that you are trying to create between you and your dog. Don't declare war over a simple mistake; he's not in the act of murdering your mother and father! Just tell him, in a calm voice, 'No, no, no, not there on the carpet, young man, you should ask to go out!' Pick him up gently and take him outside. When he has finished, bring him back in, without a fanfare or fuss.

At first, many owners use the technique of the newspaper. When the dog crouches down, they take him onto a newspaper laid on the ground. According to the principle of chain reaction in habits, the dog ends up going to the newspaper himself when he feels the need. This technique has the disadvantage of allowing the little animal to relieve himself in the house. If, unfortunately rather late in the day, the master decides that he wants his dog to use the outside facilities, he will quickly realise that it is far easier to create good habits than change bad ones.

To eradicate the bad habit of the dog relieving himself in the house, take a few steps backwards to the time when the puppy had learned not to soil his own living space. Your pet knows perfectly well how to hold back on a limited quantity. The ideal tool is the crate, the same sort as used for air transport, to fit his size and no more than that. The idea is that the dog is unable to urinate and still have enough room to lie down to one side of the puddle.

Shut him in the crate. Then, after an hour or two, take him outside the house.

Case no. 1. He does his business nicely outside. Give him half-an-hour's freedom in the house Watch him the whole time. Then take him out again. He performs outside once more? This time give him an hour's liberty inside, still under surveillance. Then take him out. If he pees outside, he will now have the right to two hours' freedom under your roof. Little by little, increase the duration of his liberty.

Case no.2. He refuses to relieve himself outside. Bring him back inside and shut him up in the crate again. Wait an hour, then take him outside again. If he urinates outside, go back to Case no.1. If not, in the crate! One more hour. Then take him out. Give him another chance to earn a little freedom.

As long as he refuses to perform in the open air, he will stay in his confined space. Don't worry, this strong-arm treatment will not last very long. His mother already taught him how to stay clean.

You can also use the crate for the situation in which the dog floods the house in your absence. Don't give him free access to drinking-water, to avoid filling his bladder, and close the door. Don't worry; a little dog can easily stay in a transport crate for twelve hours at a stretch. When I go to San Francisco, my dog stays in his crate for twenty hours. And at the end of the journey, he doesn't seem at all worn out.

In a few days, good habits will be back in place and you won't have to shut him up when you go out; he will have re-learnt how to control himself.

The crate

This is your Fluffy's apartment. You can make a plywood container yourself. The opening should be a grill that closes with a lock. Even better, if you can manage it, is to buy an aircraft crate.

The crate has many advantages:-

- no more vandalism when you're out
- no running away

- no dirtying the house
- good safety in case of accident.

Aircraft transport crates are shock-proof. If you put your dog in his cage each time you take him in the car, you will be better protected. The crate is a much better safety tool than a car harness. The crate, with a grilled door, also works perfectly well as an outdoor kennel. Just take off the grill and put the crate underneath an overhanging roof.

The postman

Each day, the postman passes, stops... then runs away. Faced with your dog, he loses the confrontation and leaves the place, sometimes in a great hurry. He is a weak enemy. The dog, like many humans, loves a victory. Your postman bolts regularly, after every visit? Wonderful! One day or another, the dog will try and crush this weakest of links, this easy prey. So he can climb the hierarchical ladder.

Be wary if your dog barks, or gets excited, or goes towards him, even by one step, when your postman leaves. It is always at this moment that the predator's instinct is sparked off in the dog. You should react at that exact moment; 'No, that's enough, I'm going to get really annoyed!' With, if necessary, a jerk on the collar.

Your dog has to understand that the moment when the postman leaves could be very disagreeable for him, instead of a triumph for his aggressive behaviour. There are several remedies. Put his muzzle on him before the postman comes and attach the long line so you can hold him or punish him from a distance. Put him in the 'Down – stay' position when the postman is actually there. In whichever case, if your dog gets wound up when the postman comes, make sure he's far enough away from your conscientious visitor that he can't touch him!

Holes in the lawn

If your favourite companion is no friend to your lawn, you could try successively or simultaneously the following methods:-

1. Put his droppings in the holes.
2. Put several mouse-traps, set and turned upside down to avoid causing damage, there where he digs, then cover them up again with a fine layer of earth; when your dog puts one paw back on the tempting surface it will be Armageddon for him!
3. Fill each hole with earth, then put a piece of mesh over it, and fix this firmly in place with pegs. When the grass has grown well, you can remove the pegs. The mesh, interlaced with the grass roots, will stop your dog from digging in the same spot.
4. Spray an external repellant on the area destroyed, then repair it, then spray again. Be careful! Don't use this sort of repellant in the house as it smells really strong.

The fighter

Before the walk, put a muzzle on him. This will prevent brawling and the vet's bills that follow.

St Bernard

Teach him to obey, so that you can slip a muzzle on him as quickly as possible. When you know how to get him to walk to heel, move towards dogs that you encounter. Watch your dog, not the others. He will see his peers before you do! If he lifts his eyes or his ears, then give a reprimand, 'Oh no, you don't!' But stop dead if he is swaggering towards them in a victorious manner. Walk backwards sharply, shaking his collar, as many times as is necessary, until your pupil is interested only in you, not in his peers. At that point, and only then, you can carry on walking straight ahead, staying alert and ready to begin again with the stop-jerk-walk backwards routine if it is necessary.

It is this walking backwards, repeated until you capture the dog's attention, that cures him of his fighting impulses. You also have to convey a physical force superior to that of your four-legged companion.

The fugitive

Physically stop him from taking French leave, by enclosing him behind strong fencing or a solid door, or by attaching him to a long chain.

Do not trust him. If you knew how many people leave their dogs free to run away then are surprised to have a fugitive pet! Without mentioning that they also go out each day, sometimes for the whole day, leaving their dog alone in an open garden...

Nowadays, there are many excellent systems of electric barrier, with and without wiring, that truly prevent the dog running away, while leaving all exits open, and that don't prevent the passage of vehicles, or people, or animals that are not fitted with a control.

These controls are quite expensive and you might prefer the trolley system; a horizontal cable, at a height of two or three metres, along which runs a chain. Attach your dog to the bottom end of this. The trolley gives the animal a good enough range of movement.

On the training side, create sources of interest for your dog directed *inside* the house. For instance, you could try putting his food bowl behind the door, at different times of day. It will always be there, but hiding sometimes. This doesn't work if your dog has little appetite. Or if you live beside a restaurant!

Don't give in, don't accept that he runs away. Lie in wait for him in places he usually passes on his way out. Watch out, his sense of smell is extraordinary.

Each fugitive dog is an individual case. Be smarter than he is! It's now or never.

And reward him richly when he ends up coming back. He must love coming home. Don't punish him when you see him again. It's your fault he ran away, so punish yourself. Anyway, it will certainly be you who feels remorse if your dog is knocked down and killed by a car.

The dog that jumps on people

When he tries to put his paws on your clean clothes:-

1. Catch hold of his paws.
2. Hold him in this position, long enough to annoy him. He will complain, throw a tantrum, argue about it.
3. At the moment when you think the punishment has lasted for long enough, release him.
4. Do this again each time he re-offends.
5. You can then increase the punishment. Instead of simply holding his front paws, tap his supporting claws on the ground with your foot.
6. Extreme measures; take away the ground beneath his feet. Without brutality of course – don't break anything! – simply push your feet under his and let him go the moment he loses his balance.

You can just as easily take out his supporting feet from under him, from behind, when he jumps on one of your visitors. Dogs retain this lesson quickly.

Refusing food

1. Only let him eat exclusively from his food bowl.

2. Ask your bit-part actors to offer him a treat. If he accepts even the tiniest piece, your friends then give a good tap on the muzzle! This time, they're allowed. It is a necessary exercise, in the interest of perhaps even saving your dog's life. And it's not you that's hitting him.
3. Put some food on the ground where your dog is going to pass it. With the animal on the lead, when he puts his muzzle near it, reprimand him strongly. Really read the riot act.

The obsessive

Castration, with a dog, doesn't work as well as with a horse. Its only certain effect is to prevent the neutered dog from reproducing!

If you have taught your dog to obey you, it is enough to tell him off when he is tempted to act on his impulses. If you have taught him the 'down-stay' he will be forced to leave dogs and people alone. And you can check out possible fiancées in the small-ads of dog magazines.

Hidden dangers

Slug-bait, anti-freeze, cans of paint, laburnum, rat-poison, dead rats and mice that were poisoned, dry thuya needles, medication in waste-bins, lawn-mowers, cars and a thousand products, plants and machines can sicken or kill the companion of all your days. Be careful!

Watch out as the hardier your dog is, the more likely he is to jump out your third floor window to pass the time of day with a passing cat.

There is no such thing as an intelligent accident…

Always have on you the telephone number of a 24 hour veterinary service. And you can dial 112, which connects to the emergency services, including those for dogs, anywhere in the world.

CHAPTER 10

Specialist training

'The master should always aim to give his pupils balanced personalities and not to turn them into specialists'

ALBERT EINSTEIN

Advanced training comes after a basic education. Until now, I've dealt with starting off and consolidating learning, the practice of the basics. The initial phases of learning are considered with experience to be fairly tedious, and sometimes downright off-putting, but they are necessary.

It is now time to move on to high school, the most inspiring. This is where the dog learns precise work; protection, hunting, tracking, flyball and plenty of other activities. This opens up canine leisure pursuits, initiation into the various dog sports, and allows a special quality of understanding to develop between dog and master.

You could one day feel like enrolling your favourite companion in these intelligent activities that are so well adapted to his deepest nature.

Your dog is starting to obey you regularly? You could of course stop there and consider that you've achieved what you set out to do.

All the same, your four-footed companion fills everyone around you with admiration. He is obedient almost to the flick of a finger-tip or raise of an eyebrow? In fact, you are already at the stage of reaping the first harvest. It would be a pity not to take things further. In this way, you feel the birth in you of a very serious disease; a passion for the working dog. The pages that follow are concerned with the stage post-training.

After puppy pre-school, after basic canine education, here are some techniques for advanced training.

The principle of learning technique for the dog is incredibly simple. It is enough to get the dog to carry out an activity, guiding him with precision, and to lavish praise on him when he succeeds, until this act becomes automatic. He will make it part of his own way of life and will even build it into his personality.

One question:-

- do you carefully make your four-footed companion lie down at the foot of the front passenger seat each time you get in the car?
- do you forbid him to move from that specific place without authorisation?
- does he receive plenty of rewards when he stays there?
- so do you have any reason to think he'd demand to get into the back seat?

From his point of view, getting in the car means lying down by the front passenger seat, full stop.

I'll say again that everything is a question of precision, tenacity and patience. The day will come, very soon, on which, when you open the door of your vehicle, the dog will lie down of his own accord on the car-mat, at the foot of the front passenger seat. That day, it will be enough just to say, in front of other people, 'In your place!' before he gets in the car. You won't be risking any setback. Your pupil will go to his place of his own accord, from habit. You'll remember to reward him, 'Good dog!' And everyone there will say that you are a genius in training dogs!

There are already many jobs for dogs and people never cease to invent new ones. For each of these training techniques that follow, I will give instructions on how you can carry them out if you want to try for yourself. The first results come very quickly for simple activities, more slowly if, for example, it's a question of training a dog as an aid for a deaf person.

From now on, you will create your own routes, along which you will progress according your own taste and at your own pace. You could equally make use of the services of a specialist. You will often have doubts, and many of them. Various adages can sustain you when you feel discouraged:-

- Think twice, not once.
- Work with logical methods.
- Apply a technique only if you believe in it.
- Don't change the method every day.
- And remember that the dog does not work to give pleasure to his master but to give pleasure to himself.

Pit-bull

When nothing is working any more, stop everything and reflect. First decide on the solution you intend to follow from now on. Make sure you're convinced that it is good, that it satisfies your dog's need for pleasure. Keep to this new formula for at least a few weeks, enough time for the first interesting effects to manifest themselves.

It is best to seek and listen to advice from everyone, from the great practitioners and from beginners, then to choose whatever suits you best.

If the results of your technique are good, so much the better. If not, change methods, either completely or partially. Man also makes progress by way of trial, success and error.

Having established that, there are certainly methods which work well for most dogs. Here they are.

Tracking

All dogs, without exception, can practise tracking. I go so far as to claim that this is the most interesting of all the disciplines. As we've seen, smell is the best of all the dog's senses. So this is what you develop further in your four-footed friend.

Explanations on how the dog's sense of smell functions vary tremendously. You can train your dog for tracking without special knowledge but here is a little theory.

Afghan Hound

In the eyes of most dog-trainers, it is through the muzzle that the dog takes in air. This is warmed up again by going through the nasal passages and then arouses various cells, which transmit this information to the brain, processed by specific nerves. However, for some tracking specialists, the route taken by the air is the reverse; the dog inhales through his mouth and exhales through his nose. Whatever the truth, whether he smells while breathing in or breathing out, the result is the same.

The anatomical perception doesn't allow us to establish any certainties. At the base of the tube that is all the muzzle really is, you'll find the vomeronasal organ, as if it's placed on a shelf. This organ goes from the root of the muzzle right to the middle of the second premolar. This little tubular canal possesses olfactory cells and 608 nervous vessels directly linked to the olfactory lobe in the brain. The nasal passage and ethmoids are responsible for fanning the air to make sure that odorous particles really make contact with the mucous, the 'olfactory epithelium', that lines the interior of the muzzle and the sinus. The olfactory nerves that go to the brain also start in this mucous.

The olfactory cells pierce the mucous, always moist, and, with their filaments, they palpate and identify particular smells.

Once more, several theories clash here. Doctor Amoore defends stereochemical theory. In an earlier time, he classified all known bodies, according to the shapes of their molecules:-

- spheres, like camphor
- egg shapes, like ether
- cones, like mint
- disks, like musk
- and disks with tails, like floral scent

He discovered that spicy or sickening smells have no specific molecular form. They differ from the others because of their respective electrical charges.

Starting from the premise that molecules have specific shapes, he imagined the theory of 'the lock and the key'; each olfactory cell would also have a particular shape, adapted to the shape of one of these families of odours, and the diverse quantities of cells of the same type, aroused at the same moment, would determine the precise identification of the odour.

Until now, there has been no proof to support Dr Amoore's concept, even if research on molecular structure seems to back him up.

Dr Wright, on the other hand, thinks that different molecules modify the natural electrical vibration of the olfactory cells. This modification would thus represent their signature, which would go towards the brain via the olfactory nerves. He christened this concept the 'theory of vibration'.

Researchers have dreamed up more than thirty theories, which all relate more or less to the two set out here. It is also possible that the theories of Wright and Amoore are more complementary than in competition. Perhaps some molecules obey the stereochemical theory and others the vibrations theory. Only the future and nature know the truth of the matter!

Resources

You will need:-

1. a long line of 10 metres, in leather or cotton or synthetic fabric. The best material is that used by sailors for their racing mainsails; drip-dry double-stranded rope, fine, strong, and rot-proof, that you will find on dogmasters.com
2. Gloves. You will understand why on the day that this rope slips through your hands at top speed.
3. A clip of the type known as a pump with besel that allows for ultra-quick attachment. Giant size ones are better as they can take very strong pressure.
4. A harness, preferably made to measure. There again, it makes no difference whether you choose leather or strapping, but this time choose one with a good width, at least 2cm, as this is clearly more comfortable for the dog. As to the model, there is really only one that is suitable in every way, and that is the Swiss harness, which lowers the dog's head while he is working.
5. In the end, you're the one who knows your dog, and you watch him mature. Take note of the toy that he likes to take in his mouth. From time to time, hide this object. It is good that your dog doesn't tire of it.

In this way, for a modest amount, you have all the basic resources needed.

Later on, and, depending on your progress, you could need pegs, flags, a pair of binoculars or a telescope, walkie talkie radios between the tracker, that is to say whoever follows your trail, and you, and – why not! – a radio-collar to communicate at a distance with your dog.

But we haven't reached all that yet!

Some important principles

It is in your interest to carry out your first attempts at tracking in a peaceful place, in normal weather conditions, to avoid your pupil being distracted. From the same perspective, first make short, straight, tracks into or across the wind direction. Don't try to do more than one or two training sessions per day. Beware the famous 'fatigue threshold'. If you overdo it you will wreck everything.

Greyhounds

Next, raise the level of difficulty in very small increments; longer tracks, in livelier places, stronger winds, tighter and tighter angles or even strange tracks put in the animal's path. Don't hesitate to go back a few steps if your dog seems unhappy during a few sessions sharpening up his skills. But don't put up with him letting things go, from laziness. The fine line between the two isn't always easy to judge.

Work frequently! You can do this alone, without help. You will learn to read your animal better and better, as long as you often practise tracking. And then again, it will also do you good to get out into the tilled fields, the vineyards, the woods and the marshes, whatever the weather!

The two principle methods

Two philosophies govern learning to track;

1. Searching for the master, then of another human.
2. Retrieving an object.

There is no conflict between these two types, quite the contrary. An effective dog should know how to use both techniques. Quite simply, each handler can, according to taste, press either button to set things in motion.

First method; finding a person

The dog, on lead, is held back by a helper. You hide. The helper lets go of the dog.

The first time, the distance should not exceed 10 metres. Little by little, take to the field. Be careful to hide at ground level; that way the dog will learn to keep his nose to the ground.

At the moment you go off to hide, call your dog. Usually, he will be champing at the bit to join you. The helper then blocks the dog's eyes and ears by placing herself between you and the dog. You go to your hiding place, dragging your feet to help both the dog and the helper. Your track will be easier to scent and more visible.

When you are in position, the helper should begin to move forward, slowly, with the dog on a long lead, and she should act as if she herself is tracking; she should sniff noisily, nose to the ground, encouraging the dog all the time, 'Search, good dog, search, well done!' After a few steps, if the dog seems to have set off well, the helper drops the long line. Her rôle is quite simple; if the dog moves forward, she stops and if the dog stops, she moves forward.

Celebrate your dog's arrival, but wait until he touches you before you move; his vision is so poor that you can't guarantee he has seen you, even if he looks in your direction.

This technique is very motivating for the dog.

Second method; retrieving an object

Before the first session, confiscate your dog's favourite toy; your work will be made easier by the fact that he has already enjoyed finding this object! Now it has to be kept for tracking exercises.

Secure your dog by attaching his lead to a fixed point. Then get his favourite toy out of your pocket, with a sneaky look. Walk backwards, murmuring, 'Watch this now, young man, your object, watch the object now, the object…', go about ten metres away and then put the toy down on the ground, behind a clump of grass, so the animal will be obliged to search until the last minute.

In a straight line, so as not to multiply tracks, go back to your starting point, but in silence. Without a word, release the dog, saying gently to him, 'Search, go on then, good dog, search…' Go with him, discreetly.

As in the search for the master, you should stop if your dog goes forward and advance if he stops. Keep a pre-occupied air, stare at the ground, sniff while leaning over, as if you feel total empathy with him, while he hasn't found his toy. When he discovers it, congratulate him.

At the beginning, don't demand that he brings you the object. The principle is that he has found it. Afterward, he should bring it to you. This requires a certain affection for the object.

There exist three main methods; play, constraint and competition. Everyone knows the game of 'Fetch', where you throw a ball further and further away, then into more and more impossible places, then throw it again when the dog brings it back. This solution presents many advantages. It satisfies the need for pleasure, it can be done with puppies and it maintains the ideal man-dog relationship.

The wise master knows to stop the session before the dog gets bored with the object.

On the other hand, nothing guarantees that the dog will always go and fetch what you want. If, somewhere along the road, he discovers a new source of interest, more appetising, he will say goodbye to the ball with no regrets.

After the game, you still need to move onto a period of constraint. The long line remains the tool of choice for control from a distance. Throw a different object, then make the dog fetch it.

If you call on constraint in the first place, command your dog to sit in the corner of a room and bring a piece of wood, the size of a biro, close to his muzzle. Say, 'Bring it here!'

At the same moment, place the object in the animal's maw, whether he's willing or not. He is sitting in his corner and can't dodge. When he has the piece of wood between his teeth, close his muzzle with one hand and release the pressure little by little. Close his muzzle again if he looks as if he's going to spit out the object. When you can see that he's going to keep it, remove your hands. Then take back the piece of wood, saying, 'Thank you!'

Little by little, demand that he brings his muzzle forward to accept the object. Bring this nearer to the ground. You will have won the day the dog goes to fetch any object on command. It's easy to say, sometimes a long time to achieve. This rigorous and effective method weighs in as rather authoritarian.

The competition method allies the advantages of both the two preceding methods, without suffering their disadvantages. Wait until the dog, or puppy, shows a preference for one toy. A shoe, for example. Attach the animal to a peg, then, very obviously, go two metres away, playing with the toy all the time. The dog will be raring to go, tugging at the end of his lead, 'What? You have the nerve to steal my toy and play with it without me?'

Go back without saying a word and release the dog. He will hurl himself towards the object. Follow him quickly but, at the moment he is just about to seize the shoe, confiscate it in front of him. Put it in your pocket, the session is over.

After a few days, the animal, tormented with the desire to recover his possession before anyone else, has no difficulty in launching himself at the command, 'Search and fetch!' Place the toy further and further away. Put it fifty metres away. Make sure you move ahead, at the same time as you release the dog. He knows that, if he doesn't get to the object before you, he's lost. When he has seized the shoe in his mouth, give the command, 'Heel!' He knows to come back. 'Sit!' He knows to sit.

The sole weakness of this technique is that the dog doesn't like giving up his prey. A little authority can be enough but a treat as reward, in the form of a cube of cheese for instance, can resolve this difficulty even better.

Another reward; throw the object again after you've reclaimed it. Little by little, your dog will give it back to you of his own accord for you to throw it again for him more quickly. Dogs, in general, love this game.

German pointer

Learning to swim

Many dogs don't like swimming. Nevertheless, it is excellent exercise. If your dog shows himself to be dead set against the liquid element, this is how to proceed.

On a lovely summer's day, go and paddle with him in a clean pool with plenty of shallows that you can stand in. Go in front, holding him by the lead. Go into the water and he'll follow, because of the lead. Congratulate him warmly when he loses his footing and starts to swim.

If you know how to swim, nothing is better than example. Take hold of the long line, go into the water yourself and call the animal to you when you are already some way from the edge. Here, the long line will force him to join you once more.

If you don't want to get sopping wet, ask a friend to go with you down to a small river. Ask her to hold your dog, to which you've attached a long line. Hold the line at its longest, go to the other bank of the river. Call your dog. If he doesn't come, pull, gently on your long line, without releasing it. The dog will end up going into the water. Reward him when he comes towards you.

If you are on your own, pass a long cord over to the other side of the river, behind a tree trunk, but keep hold of both ends. Attach them to a secure collar on the dog, which is still beside you. Then pull on one of the two ends of rope, letting the other run. In this way, you're forcing the dog to move towards the water, 'Come on then! In you go!' Stop pulling if he moves forward of his own accord. Call him back when you like but he should continue to move forward as long as he doesn't hear the recall command.

With time, the animal comes to understand that there is nothing frightening about water, and that, all in all, he can even have some fun there.

Agility

This sport, originating in Britain, is a form of show-jumping for dogs. They have to pass over or through various obstacles – beams, see-saws, tunnels, hedges, bars and a slalom – in the shortest possible time.

This leisure activity lets your dog stretch his legs and teaches him not to be afraid of obstacles. According to your own taste, you can dream up ways of incorporating all sorts of natural pitfalls into your daily walk; a stream to cross or a felled tree trunk. The training principle is simple. During such an active walk, choose an interesting obstacle, a command adapted to that obstacle, and, repeating the command throughout the exercise, guide your dog through the activity.

For example, a felled tree trunk goes across a dry stream-bed. Say, 'Over, over, over' At the same time, guide your pupil along the trunk while you walk alongside it. When the dog reaches the far side of the dry river bed, at the other end of the trunk, release him and praise him warmly.

Don't give up half-way. Your dog is not allowed to escape by getting down from the trunk before the end.

For a jump, use the command, 'Jump!' for a tunnel, 'Through!' for a table, 'Under!' for a slalom, 'Zigag!'

Your dog will love these games if you remember to reward him for every success. One day, it will be enough to show him an obstacle, give him a suitable order and he will carry out the work of his own accord.

You could also join an agility club.

The protection dog

'God gave man the dog for company and protection,' Denis Diderot

All our dogs can defend us by biting, from the little Yorkshire terrier to the great St Bernard. But this action should be limited to only instances of legitimate defence.

To establish legitimate defence, you need the following conditions:-

1. the existence of an aggression.
2. the aggression should be unprovoked.
3. the defence should take place simultaneously with the aggression.
4. the defence should be proportional to the nature and gravity of the aggression.

If your dog removes three fingers from some stranger who asks you for a light, you will find it difficult to argue for legitimate defence. On the other hand, if your dog took a chunk out of someone's thigh when this person broke into your house through a window, at midnight, armed, the law will uphold you completely.

Legitimate defence can equally be applied to protecting your own dog from attack by others. But, as always, it's a good idea to keep your cool as much as possible and to let your response be proportional to the intensity of the aggression.

Ideally, you should prepare well, with your dog, by undergoing training for protection, because the best trained are always assaulted least.

In Europe, someone keen on protection dogs has a huge advantage over those wanting to practise other canine sports; there are vast numbers of specialist clubs where competent supervisors offer good quality teaching.

It's not just a sport. The army, customs, police, security services employ dogs trained to use their teeth.

Bitework contains two elements:-

1. Teaching the dog to really bite and grow in courage.
2. Learning to control the dog, even in moments when he is really furious, or when a fight has reached its height.

French bulldog

This is the reason why well-trained protection dogs generally don't have behaviour problems. Their masters push the dogs' aggressiveness to the highest levels while establishing absolute control despite everything. He who can do the most can do the least. In everyday life, these animals display very pleasant natures; they are polite, sociable, calm. They know not to chase cats.

In my view, work on biting is a martial art. 'Noblesse oblige'; nobility and responsibility. Master and dog have to acquire absolute control over their behaviour.

You teach a dog to bite via two of his sharpest instincts; his instinct for prey and his instinct for defence.

To develop his instinct for prey, take any old duster and shake it in front of his nose like a pompon at a fairgound stall. One moment or another, the dog is going to try and grab it. Let him have it. The next few days, delay a little the moment he gets his trophy.

But don't go too far in that direction. Very quickly, as soon as the dog is involved in the game, ask a helper to hold the duster. Above all, don't teach your dog to bite you!

If you want to make the most of the defence instinct, ask your helper to threaten you with gestures and aggressive words. Hold the animal back closely, your hand on his collar. At the same moment, murmur angrily, 'On guard now, my boy, watch that thug, on guard!' At the first growl from your pupil, your helper should run away. Praise your dog. Little by little, he is going to follow his instincts when he sees someone with a dubious or threatening attitude.

In addition to these two driving forces, prey and defence, you can, as in all exercises use induced training.

Go out for a walk one night in a dark place. While on his lead, does the dog bark in the direction of a passing silhouette? Tell him, 'Well done, tiger, on guard!'

In this, more than in any other discipline, it really is in your interest to put all the techniques to work. You know that, according to the phenomenon of the resultant of excitations, the different methods multiply their effects.

Activating the prey instinct is perfectly conceivable with a puppy. Just be careful not to make unreasonable physical demands on your young pupil. In particular, avoid making him bite during the period that he is losing his milk teeth.

On the other hand, if you resort to the defence instinct too often, you will ruin the animal. At what age can you start? That depends on the dog. I've seen fox-terrier puppies shake a linen bolster like a plum-tree and 18 month old German Shepherd Dogs that hid behind their masters' legs when a stranger came towards them.

These things are sensed; if the animal seems tough enough, risk a session with a helper. Make your mind up depending on how well that manoeuvre goes.

Stopping a dog biting doesn't necessarily imply the use of force. Plenty of dogs will accept letting go and coming back when you simply call them to heel, 'Wolf, come here, my brave dog!'

However, even if the learning has taken place in the right conditions, despite everything, you still run the risk of suffering a refusal to obey. Biting is just too exciting for him to stop after the first seconds of making contact. You need therefore to make use of a tool the animal already knows well, an escalation of the 'ringing bell'. This is none other than a variation on the theme of recall to heel using the long line, an exercise already covered in detail. With a particularly combative pupil, the master sometimes has to be prepared to act vigorously to demand the release of the prey. If you feel yourself physically or mentally unable to use force to make your pupil obey you, it is probably better to forget any idea of working a defence dog. The animal would very rapidly become a menace to everyone around him.

Once biting and stopping are established, you move on to the dog's capacity to read meetings intelligently.

The dog is expected to stay calm and approachable when someone inoffensive comes to greet the handler or to shake his hand. He should place himself on guard, or give a warning, if someone, still inoffensive, merely comes close, and he should respond by attacking, without any command needed, if an aggressor touches his master.

Everyone understands that this intelligence when someone approaches is not achieved with a dog that's out of control. Driven by the desire to bite, your pupil must know how to hold back. This canine self-control is a quality eminently useful in everyday life. Unless you are a security guard, there is no daily need to be defended by your dog. Especially when there is such a powerful dissuasion to attack walking everywhere at your side.

The protection dog is above everything a subordinate animal; he fears nothing and nobody, except his master!

He also knows how to race to attack an individual. This frontal attack is most debutants' dream, as they consider it the epitome of the idea of defence. But it is just the beginning. Two points indicate perfect training; a halt in mid-flight at any

Basset Hound

moment, and a stop to the biting with a return at the gallop to the master. To obtain this, the long line is the most certain means of control.

Clearly, the decoy, in a padded outfit, plays a fundamental rôle here. It is up to him to develop the animal's courage, then to provoke mistakes, without ever breaking his dynamism.

In all bitework, the decoy behaves as rather more than a simple clothes-horse. He takes a full part in the training. A true accomplice for the master, he should possess great technical skills. If you take with you some lame duck, or foul-mouthed hooligan, then you will run into setbacks straight away. Goodbye precision, goodbye progress, goodbye pleasure.

Biting attacks are carried out on a man who squares up or runs away. In the exercise of finding a wrong-doer in disguise, the dog finds the man, doesn't bite, but barks a warning and a signal to make his master come.

All canine sports, practised according to the agreed rules, offer great pleasure, to the masters as to the dogs. I can never advise people too often that they should work in at least one canine discipline. And I know that the most well-balanced dogs are those that take part in many!

Conclusion

'Flatter your dog. If you don't know why, he does'

MICHEL HASBROUCK

Not really to conclude an infinite subject but to offer some essential advice:-

- Always be accessible to your dog. Keep your conversations with him simple, clear, uncluttered. When he does well, reward him warmly. But if you have to punish him, do so with a clear conscience.
- Don't give contradictory commands. How many times have I seen owners command 'Come on, down, come on, down!' then 'Come here, let's go then, come here!' Then 'Come on then, let's go and play!' Whether they want to elicit a recall, a 'down' or send the dog away, they say 'come on then' with no distinction. Put yourself in the place of the poor animal. What can he understand of these humans who pronounce the same words when giving three very different orders? Be careful; 'Come!' is an order. 'Go!' is an order. 'Come on, let's go!' is two orders. And contradictory ones. Choose! If you want Trixie to come, then say only, 'Come!' or 'Come here!' If you want her to go, say 'Go!' And for the 'down' restrain yourself to asking, 'Down!'
- Don't trust yourself; *'Any man invested with authority has the tendency to abuse it,' Lawrence J Peter*. Don't give too many commands. No more than one command per hour. Be careful; an hour is a long time. If you don't know what to say to your dog, send him a compliment. 'You're gorgeous, you great hairy beast, you.'
- Never forget; reward your dog when he has made an effort.

Unfortunately, a dog that behaves well and that controls himself, is not spectacular. It is easy for the master to forget to show his satisfaction. And then the dog feels misunderstood and not trusted.

From now on, on the contrary, whatever the place, whatever the time, tell him as often as possible, 'Well done, my dog, that's great!' With warmth, in a sweet, loving voice. You will tell me that you do give your dog lots of compliments. I will reply, 'Not enough!' Starting from today, your animal should receive more compliments than his usual ration.

English Cocker Spaniel

Tell him, 'Well done, fluffball, well done garbage bin, well done, my cookie monster, my party animal,' each time that he looks at you with those brimming calf-eyes. For me, all the training is just a pretext to create opportunities for rewards.

We talk about catching your dog's eye. While he is concentrating on you, your dog is much more attentive to your instructions. To reach this 'state of grace' all you need to do, believe me, is to say something nice to him at the moment he is looking at you, then at the moment he does something good, Be careful! It's more difficult than it sounds. But when the dog concentrates on his master, the game is won.

Use more kind words, so easy to give lavishly. Cut down on

the importance of caresses. It is a real palaver, a caress; you have to move, stop what you're doing for long enough… All in all, you don't give many in the course of a day. And there again, the caress, that stereotypical gesture, doesn't allow for much fine-tuning of feelings. Of course, it does correspond to our materialist philosophy as we feel impelled to give palpable presents. But our dogs are not like humans, attached to things.

Your voice is an incredibly valuable tool. It offers you a palette of infinite variations to use in your communication with your four-footed friend. You can easily give plenty of compliments, of kind words. Personally, I love sweet nothings, said in a low voice, purring, that automatically attract my dog's attention.

You can choose which words to use. When someone pays you a compliment, that gives you pleasure, doesn't it? Then why would you think that your dog is insensible? And, admit it, as working principles go, there are more unpleasant philosophies…

Our Website

You will find all the products necessary for dog-training and for looking after your dog in the Dogbaggy (not doggybag!) on dogmasters.com. Catalogue available free from

Michel Hasbrouck service LED

Maison forestière de la jumelle

78690 Les-Essarts-le-Roi, France

(Don't forget to give your address and enough stamps/international reply coupons to cover postage)

You will also find the catalogue on my site www.dogmasters.com

Don't hesitate to consult the website. Besides a wealth of specialist information, with free advice about breeding (from a breeder), behaviour (from a dog-trainer), animal health (from a veterinary surgeon), legislation (from a barrister), pet insurance (from an insurer) and security (from a police officer). A wide-ranging menu of articles and approved services completes what is on offer.

The dog in the act of tracking

Holding the long line to stop a dog pulling, the surplus over his back

Holding a handle-less lead

Touching the back paws of a dog that's jumping

Trapping the lead in a doorway to keep the dog in the car

The dog on cross-country

Natural agility courses

The kong, a dog's favourite toy

The zoomgroom brush, that grooms without hurting